Proposal Writing
The Art of Friendly Persuasion

William S. Pfeiffer
SOUTHERN COLLEGE OF TECHNOLOGY

MERRILL PUBLISHING COMPANY
A Bell & Howell Information Company
Columbus Toronto London Melbourne

To the memory of my parents,
Hal and Jean Pfeiffer

Published by Merrill Publishing Company
A Bell & Howell Information Company
Columbus, Ohio 43216

This book was set in Palatino.

Administrative Editor: John Yarley
Production Coordinator: Molly Kyle
Art Coordinator: Ruth Kimpel
Cover Design Coordinator: Brian Deep
Text Designer: Connie Young

Library of Congress Catalog Card Number: 88-61090
International Standard Book Number: 0-675-20988-9
Printed in the United States of America
1 2 3 4 5 6 7 8 9—93 92 91 90 89

PREFACE

Everyone who writes in school or on the job must *sell*. Forget about academic distinctions between persuasive writing and so-called objective writing; the fact is that all writing has three persuasive goals.

- To capture the reader's interest
- To show your credibility
- To sell a particular product, service, or idea

Although principles of persuasion apply to everything you write, their importance is most obvious in one particular form of job-related writing: the proposal.

Despite their importance, proposals do not get the attention they deserve. In the case of sales proposals, you may face strict and sometimes unrealistic deadlines imposed by clients and colleagues. In the case of in-house proposals, you usually must add the time for them to your already heavy workload. These time constraints affect quality. Use this handbook, therefore, for quick and simple guidelines and models—whether to prepare a class assignment or to write a professional proposal.

Whether you are enrolled in school or starting a new job, you will spend a lot of time writing—essays, research papers, routine letters, memos, and reports. As you move up the job ladder, however, you will begin to write proposals as well, and these three points will become obvious to you:

If you want your ideas or needs to get attention from managers, you need to put them in writing. Ideas are cheap, but a proposal shows your commitment.

As you move toward management positions yourself, you will spend most of your time writing persuasively, both to subordinates and superiors.

> In a competitive business, career advancement usually brings with it more responsibility for writing sales proposals to customers.

In short, as you move from entry-level positions into management, proposal writing comes with the territory. Since you won't be able to escape it, learn to do it well. This book will help you reach that goal.

Proposal Writing takes you through the entire proposal cycle, from first contact to last follow-up letter. Because winning proposals rely on effective writing and speaking, you will find suggestions both for writing and for oral presentations. Most importantly, the book provides excellent models to follow as you prepare written and spoken presentations. These are the book's main features:

- Overviews of both marketing and writing processes
- Guidelines for writing letters and proposals
- Suggestions for improving interpersonal skills
- Examples, with critiques, to use as models
- Realistic exercises
- A descriptive list of additional readings

You will find practical, everyday use for this book when you write letters before and after the proposal and the proposal itself, and when you participate in personal meetings, formal presentations, and negotiations. The lists of guidelines and real-life models will aid your proposal effort from start to finish.

The ten chapters move through all stages of the proposal process from planning through the final presentation. Yet each chapter is self-contained so you can go directly to the specific material you need, without having to review other chapters. Chapter 1, The Marketing Process, puts proposals in the context of building long-term relationships with managers and clients. Chapter 2 surveys the main stages in the writing process—planning, drafting, and editing—and describes the "storyboarding" technique. Chapter 3 explains when and how to write letters that go before and after sales proposals and contains four letter models.

Chapters 4, 5, and 6 teach you how to write three kinds of proposals and give you samples of each—formal sales proposals, informal sales proposals, and in-house proposals. Chapter 7 shows how to effectively use visual aids in proposals, including tables and six types of charts, while Chapter 8 describes the editing process and lists guidelines for style, grammar, and proofreading.

Chapters 9 and 10 give information about related topics—making oral presentations and conducting and participating in meetings and negotiations. The Appendix is an annotated bibliography of further readings on proposals.

For survival, both working professionals and college students have a vested interest in the proposal process. One group already inhabits a world in which successful proposals mean staying in business; the other will soon join that world. This handbook, then, is designed for use by three different groups:

> *College students* whose instructors assign the book for technical writing, management communication, or proposal writing courses.
>
> *Working professionals* who want to read the entire book as a refresher or who need an easy-to-read desk guide—both for the sales and in-house proposal process.
>
> *Instructors in colleges and in companies* who need a text for courses on proposals, sales letters, proposal presentations, or negotiating.

Whatever your present role, this book will make you more skilled in the art of friendly persuasion.

Acknowledgments

First, I'd like to thank all the companies with whom I've worked as a writing consultant; that "in the trenches" experience has given me most of my ideas about proposal writing. In particular, McClelland Engineers of Houston, Texas, gave me the chance to spend six enjoyable years in the real world of report and proposal writing.

My appreciation also goes to the many students at Southern Tech who, like my friends in industry, worked hard to put writing rules into practice. Several of these students kindly allowed me to use their work as the basis for examples developed in this text; I especially thank Sam Rundell, David Cox, and Rob Duggan. I would also like to thank these reviewers for their helpful comments: Jackie Zrubek, Texas State Technical Institute–Waco; Thomas Clark, University of Nevada–Las Vegas; and Rita Bova, Columbus State Community College.

I owe my greatest debt to Evelyn Hepp Pfeiffer, who offered solid suggestions based on many careful readings of the manuscript, and to Zach and Katie Pfeiffer, who loved me in spite of this time-consuming project.

CONTENTS

PART ONE

OVERVIEW OF THE PROPOSAL PROCESS

Usually, proposals that fail (1) have been written in isolation, with too little knowledge of the reader's real needs, and (2) reflect little concern for the entire writing process of planning, drafting, and editing.

You can avoid the first error by viewing the proposal as just one part of a long-term effort. The goal is to build close relationships with the managers or clients you want to influence. You can avoid the second error by understanding and then completing all three stages of the writing process. Toward this end, this first section of the book

○ Places writing in the context of the entire communication cycle with your reader

○ Surveys the three-stage process in producing any sales document

Specifically, Chapter 1 focuses on the need to build trust through frequent contacts—in writing, by phone, and in person. The reader's familiarity with you creates respect for your abilities as a communicator, as well as an interest in what you intend to propose. Chapter 1 describes the cycle of contacts for two main types of proposals: sales proposals and in-house proposals. In this way the first chapter explores the marketing context for all sales writing.

Chapter 2 gives an overview of the process for writing any important document and answers questions like these:

○ How do you know what the reader really wants?

○ Are outlines necessary?

○ How can you cut your writing time?

○ What is an all-purpose plan of organization?

○ Does "style" really matter?

Chapter 2 provides a general foundation for the specific writing guidelines contained in Chapter 3 (Sales Letters), Chapter 4 (Formal Sales Proposals), Chapter 5 (Informal Sales Proposals), and Chapter 6 (In-house Proposals). It also introduces the editing process that will be covered in Chapter 8 (Editing).

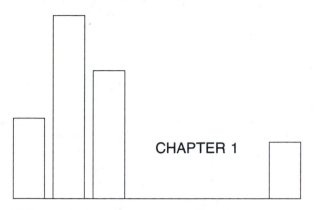

CHAPTER 1

The Marketing Process

OBJECTIVES

- ○ Understand the importance of building strong personal relationships with those to whom you write proposals
- ○ Learn how to cement the bond between you and the readers of your external sales proposal
- ○ Learn how to cement the bond between you and the readers of your in-house proposal
- ○ Do exercises to reinforce the significance of this relationship-building

On a beautiful Saturday afternoon, Max Smith is washing his car in his driveway. Halfway through the job, his next-door neighbor's daughter, an assertive ten-year-old, walks over to the edge of the drive. Susie has magazine brochures in one hand and a pencil in the other, so Max quickly surmises that it's time once again for the school's annual fund-raising drive. Although he already receives more magazines than he can possibly read, Max finds himself cheerfully ordering two more subscriptions. After all, Susie needs just ten more sales to earn a cassette tape-player for top salesperson of the week!

Let's analyze this sale. Why was Max such a pushover? He regularly turns down phone solicitations for magazines and tears up magazine sweepstakes mail without even opening it. The answer, of course, is that he *knows* Susie and her parents. He'll buy the same product from his neighbors that he would not consider buying from someone he didn't know.

This book starts with the simple principle evident in Max Smith's purchase. Your proposals are most successful when you've gotten to know your audience. *Getting to know your proposal readers means discovering and then satisfying their deep-felt needs.* This goal is the stuff of long-term trust building. Indeed, it supplies the driving force behind all proposal writing.

This book assumes that your proposals aim to satisfy the needs of (1) clients outside your firm, to whom you propose a product, service, or idea, or (2) managers in your own organization, to whom you propose in-house changes. In either case, you need to be interested in the long-term goal of building good relationships and securing repeat business from a satisfied audience.

Building Personal Relationships

Whatever product, service, or idea you're selling, remember that your goal is to strengthen personal relationships. This process relies on the strategy of establishing a pattern of repeated and helpful contacts with the people you are trying to influence. Some contacts are quite personal, as in meetings or phone conversations, while others, such as letters, are less so. All of them work together to convince your clients or your managers that you can satisfy a need.

You should view the proposal process as a continuum of contacts with your audience. This process begins with your first meeting, phone call, or letter and ends with the last thank-you letter or project report. The "end" of the relationship is only temporary, of course, since successful projects and strong working relationships will lead to more work.

We will outline two communication cycles. One applies to your clients and thus to sales proposals; the other applies to your managers and thus to in-house proposals. The key to your success with proposals is your persistence in following through on *all* these steps.

The Sales Proposal Process: Twelve Steps to Success

All salespeople know that customers want good, old-fashioned service. No matter what specific approach to marketing you may take, your success depends on giving your clients the personal attention they deserve. Excellent service means being there, ready to help your clients analyze and then solve their problems. As a reward, you establish a strong bond with them. It is this long-term relationship that all really successful companies seek. Your proposals have a much better chance when directed to someone who already respects your work, rather than to a new client. As shown in Figure 1-1, there are twelve steps that will help cement the bond with your client and generate repeat business. These steps are grouped into four stages:

○ Stage #1: Breaking In
○ Stage #2: Getting Known
○ Stage #3: Clinching the Job
○ Stage #4: Following Through

Although the most likely context for this process is a solicited (requested) sales proposal, the list can easily be adjusted to accommodate a proposal

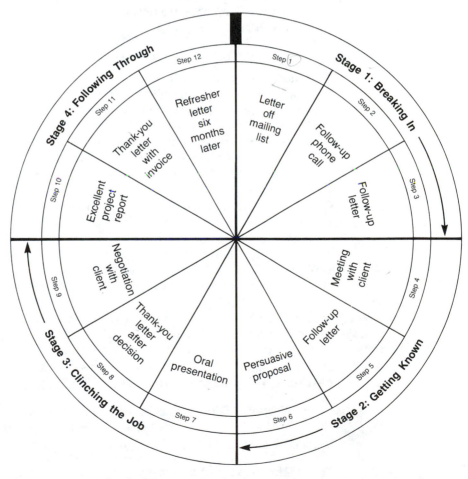

FIGURE 1–1 Wheel of Fortune: Twelve Steps in the Sales Proposal Process

that is unsolicited (not requested). Chapters 3, 4, and 5 give detailed guidelines for writing the sales letters and proposal mentioned in these steps.

Step #1: Send a letter to someone on a mailing list.

On a scale of one to ten, these types of letters score barely a "1" for effectiveness in relationship building; however, they're a necessary start if you have no previous contact with the client.

Your first letter needs only to get the client's interest by drawing attention to some need; it does not need to "sell" anything. Chapter 3 offers suggestions for writing "cold-call" letters and includes an example. For now, remember not to seek any commitment in this first letter. You're dealing with professionals who need time to evaluate you and your product or service. For example, you should avoid asking readers to return a card or form (return percentages are notoriously low). Instead, state in your letter that you will . . .

Step #2: Telephone the person to whom you send the letter.

Telephoning dramatically increases your chance of finding good leads. You become a real person to the client, not merely a purveyor of junk mail. More important, a phone conversation gives you the first opportunity to demonstrate how you can satisfy a need. Remember: *always* show yourself to be someone who is trying to help solve a problem, not just trying to sell something. In this example, the caller begins with a point that will probably catch the listener's attention: "Mr. Sampson, I mentioned in my letter that we've found a number of toxic waste sites on commercial property in Barnes County. I thought you might want to know about some of these sites, in case your bank plans to invest in that area."

The tone here is helpful, not pushy. The goal is to refresh Mr. Sampson's memory about your letter, get his interest in a topic that might concern his bank, and offer useful (and free!) information. Later in the relationship you can become specific about your firm's interest in conducting toxic waste surveys on commercial property for which Sampson's bank might provide mortgages. For the moment, however, you need to help him realize there's a problem that needs to be addressed. If the call goes well, you'll arrange a time to call back after the client has thought about what you're offering. If the call goes *really* well, you'll set up a meeting. In that case, the next relationship-building step is to . . .

Step #3: Send a letter immediately after the phone call and before your meeting.

Your letter may include some or all of these four objectives:

- o Express some excitement about the ideas the two of you discussed on the phone

- Summarize the results of the discussion
- Offer a few more ideas you've put together since the call
- Confirm the arrangements for your meeting

Again, the goal is to be seen as the "helper." You want to reinforce whatever good communication may have begun between the two of you over the phone. This letter must be in the mail right away—no later than 48 hours after the phone call. The real value of all sales letters is their *immediacy.* With the first phone call or two behind you and your follow-up letter sent, you're now ready to . . .

Step #4: Meet with the client.

This book is mainly about written and oral presentations, not interpersonal sales techniques. It's worth noting, however, that your first meeting with the client must not be a stressful or forced affair. Be a professional who has answers to problems, not a slick salesperson with a product or service to pitch. Maintain a tone and approach that demonstrate your interest in diagnosing the client's problem, without prematurely discussing what you have to sell. These sentences reflect the approach and tone you might want to adopt.

- "Mr. Sampson, are you familiar with your bank's liability if you were to foreclose on commercial property with toxic waste problems?"
- "Could you give me a few more details about the kinds of commercial property First National is interested in?"
- "What kinds of information do you now get about the use and condition of commercial property for which you might provide loans?"

Notice that these questions encourage Sampson to talk about his problems. Most potential clients will do this quickly *if* you give them the chance. You'll be listening carefully, taking notes, and generally helping to diagnose a possible problem. When it seems appropriate, of course, you can interject comments about your company's services, but only when the need for these services has been fully explored.

Successful first meetings can end in two ways. You may be fortunate enough to be asked to submit a proposal, or, more likely, you'll leave with the understanding that you are to get back to the client with further information. This approach helps you maintain control, even though the client is still undecided about your product or service. In this case, then, the next step is to . . .

Step #5: Send a letter immediately after the meeting.

A follow-up letter after your meeting will

- Summarize briefly your understanding of the conversation
- Give you the opportunity to send along a helpful item—a bro-chure, flyer, or article reprint. Don't squander these premiums by leaving them in the client's office when you visit. Save them for the follow-up letter. They'll get more attention and, of course, give you good reason to make this additional contact with the client.

At this point you may be wondering if you can overdo this business of writing letters. But remember that it's human nature to look forward to receiving first-class mail. A letter remains the cheapest, most effective way to reach the decision makers in any organization.

Having written your letter, you may engage in another series of phone calls and meetings before you receive the request for an official proposal. As we will see in Chapter 4, this request is often in the form of a *formal request for proposal* (RFP), or it may come simply in a phone call from your client asking you to send along some cost figures and rationale. Thus, your next task is to . . .

Step #6: Write a dynamic, persuasive proposal.

A pervasive theme of this book is that the proposal does not stand alone. Its success depends largely on all the relationship-building efforts that accompany it—letters, meetings, and phone calls. Yet your written proposal is certainly a focal point of the marketing process. It must be the culmination of all the phone calls, meetings, and sales letters. It must be responsive to all the reader's needs. It must, in the last analysis, stand as a statement about you as a communicator. (Chapters 4, 5, and 6 discuss guidelines for sales and in-house proposals.) If the client likes your proposal, you may be asked to . . .

Step #7: Orally present proposal highlights and answer questions.

Although most people place speech making high on their list of unpleasant tasks, Chapter 9, "Oral Presentations," will help you overcome common obstacles in this process and deliver a first-rate presentation. Here are some basic pointers:

- View the presentation as an opportunity to show the uniqueness of your proposal and to strengthen your relationship with the client.
- Adhere precisely to whatever time limits and other constraints the client has given; when in doubt, make it short.
- Send the client a letter the next day, expressing appreciation for the chance to give the presentation and summarizing its highlights.

○ Call or write to the client promptly if there are any points you promised to follow up on. You'll impress most clients by being one of the few speakers who mean it when they say "I'll get back to you on that."

At this point you've done all you can do. Soon you'll get the news that your proposal has either been accepted or rejected. In either case, plan to . . .

Step #8: Write a thank-you letter after the proposal decision.

If your proposal was rejected, a letter shows that you're a good sport, and, of course, it shows that you're interested in keeping the door open for later work. You may also want to inquire as to why your proposal was rejected or outmatched by that of your competitors. The desire to know your own deficiencies indicates to the client that you're the kind of flexible, concerned person to consider for the next contract. Remember—you're in the business of building long-term relationships, not just getting one contract.

In the case of acceptance, you of course want to express appreciation for the go-ahead decision. Your letter gives clients reinforcement that they have made the right decision. Now comes the delicate effort to . . .

Step #9: Negotiate by searching for shared interests.

Many sales arrangements require negotiations to set final terms of, for example, costs and project schedule. As will be explained in Chapter 10, this is the time to abandon old ideas about negotiating, which fortunately has progressed beyond the intimidating "I win/you lose" techniques of the past. Instead, be consistent with the tone set thus far in the proposal process by finding out what you have in common with the client. After establishing points of agreement, you're in a better psychological position to pursue areas about which there may be differences of opinion. This gentler approach to negotiating doesn't mean giving in too quickly or failing to assert yourself. Instead, it means striving to have clients view you as a colleague rather than an adversary. With negotiations completed, your next chance to strengthen your relationship with the client is to . . .

Step #10: Write an excellent project report.

Strictly speaking, reports are not part of the proposal process and thus are not covered in this text. But we must never forget that *all* business writing is persuasive; for example, progress reports must show that your project is on schedule, and final project reports must show that the entire job fulfilled the client's expectations.

Traditionally, billing the client closely follows completion of a project. It's unfortunate that the last impression your clients have of you is this request for money. One way to soften the blow of the bill is to . . .

Step #11: Send a letter of thanks with the invoice.

Rather than sending the invoice alone, show your interest in further work by enclosing a brief letter of thanks. If the invoice goes to an accounting department rather than to your contact, send a separate letter of thanks at the same time you send the invoice. Leaving clients with good feelings about your efforts will pave the way for your being selected again.

We earlier called this list of opportunities to connect with clients a "cycle." To keep good clients, you need to restart the cycle after the invoice letter; thus, you need to . . .

Step #12: Send a "refresher" letter no more than six months later.

A few months after your project, send clients a letter to refresh their memories about your services. (Perhaps you know of a new project the client plans to pursue or perhaps you have a new service to offer.) In this letter you should

- Say that you enjoyed working on the previous job
- Set the stage for a new round of meetings, phone calls, letters, and proposal

You'll always achieve the best proposal-acceptance ratios with those clients for whom you've previously done good work. Most marketing energy, therefore, should go toward getting repeat business. Then the cycle will continue.

The In-house Proposal Process: Five Steps to Success

We have seen that sales proposals result from careful attention to an entire marketing cycle. The same technique works for in-house proposals. To be sure, routine suggestions are often approved or rejected without the fanfare of a proposal or multiple contacts with managers. But once your idea moves beyond the routine, you make your best case by putting it in writing and plotting a complete internal marketing strategy. As shown in Figure 1-2, five steps can help you achieve success with your in-house proposal. (Chapter 6 gives specific writing guidelines and a model in-house proposal.)

Step #1: Run the idea past your boss.

After giving careful consideration to your idea, approach your supervisor in person to get a preliminary response. You may have some tentative ideas to present in written form—for example, a one-page outline. If your supervisor is cool toward the idea, then you can back off without having made any major investment of time. If your supervisor shows some interest, howev-

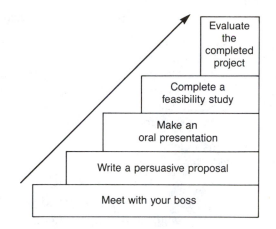

FIGURE 1–2 In-house Proposals: Five Steps to Success

er, then offer to write the proposal. Because in-house proposals often result from "inspiration" and are thus unsolicited, this one-on-one meeting helps to start your boss thinking your way and sets the stage for acceptance of your written effort.

Step #2: Write a persuasive proposal.

The proposal should follow the guidelines included in Chapter 6, unless your potential readers request another format. Before you submit it, ask several of your trusted peers to review a draft. You will probably discover that their differing views of the company's needs will lead to some useful advice. Just as important, these readers will acquire some "ownership" of the proposal. If their opinions are later sought by those charged with accepting or rejecting your proposal, you will have already developed supporters. Also, solicit opinions of any employees who will be affected by your proposal, for these reasons:

- Like the peers whose views you seek, these colleagues will provide constructive criticism.
- They will be more likely to speak favorably about your idea later during the actual review process if they've had the benefit of an early reading.

Step #3: Make an oral presentation.

Offer to meet with decision makers to:

- Present highlights of the written proposal
- Answer any questions

Step #4: Complete a feasibility study.

If the proposed project is approved but perhaps needs further research, offer to complete a feasibility study. Like both a proposal and a report, a feasibility study evaluates the practicality of doing what you have proposed. Because the project will forever be associated with your name, you want to ensure that it stands a good chance of success before you proceed. An objective, thorough feasibility study should

- Establish clear, preferably measurable, criteria by which the proposed idea can be judged
- Include cost as well as personnel requirements
- Examine several alternatives besides the preferred one
- Support the alternative that best satisfies the established criteria, even if it is not the one you originally proposed

Step #5: Evaluate the completed project.

If the feasibility study proves positive and the project goes forward, be sure to evaluate the results. This evaluation should include a written report to those who approved the proposal, so that they are aware of the success of your work. Here are some questions that your evaluation should answer.

- What were the specific objectives of the proposed project?
- What objectives were reached?
- What objectives were not reached and why?
- Was the proposed schedule followed?
- Did the project stay within its proposed budget?
- Will follow-up work be needed and who will do it?

Even if the proposal resulted in a less-than-successful project, you will usually gain respect through your willingness to evaluate the project honestly.

SUMMARY

Proposal writing is only part of the larger goal of building trusting relationships with customers and managers. You can establish this trust through a series of repeated and helpful contacts. For external sales proposals, these contacts can include these steps:

Stage #1: Breaking In

1. Send a letter to someone on a mailing list.
2. Telephone the person to whom you send the letter.
3. Send a letter immediately after the phone call.

Stage #2: Getting Known

4. Meet with the client.
5. Send a letter immediately after the meeting.
6. Write a dynamic, persuasive proposal.

Stage #3: Clinching the Job

7. Orally present highlights and answer questions.
8. Write a thank-you letter after the decision.
9. Negotiate by searching for shared interests.

Stage #4: Following Through

10. Write an excellent project report.
11. Send a letter of thanks with the invoice.
12. Send a "refresher" letter about six months later.

For internal proposals, the contacts can include these steps:

1. Meet with your boss.
2. Write a persuasive proposal.
3. Make an oral presentation.
4. Complete a feasibility study.
5. Evaluate the completed project.

Chapters 3 through 6 give detailed guidelines on the format and content of sales letters, sales proposals, and in-house proposals.

EXERCISES

1. *Sales proposal process: Real content*

   (This exercise can serve as the basis for a discussion, oral report, or written report.)

   Use company data from your own or others' work experience. Assume that (1) within the last year you decided to market a product, service, or idea to a client with whom you've never done business, and (2) you were successful in getting work with this new client. Now report on how you would have worked through the twelve-step process for sales proposals outlined in this chapter. Be specific about your objectives and techniques at each step of the process.

2. *Sales proposal process: Simulated content*

(This exercise can serve as the basis for a discussion, oral report, or written report.)

You are responsible for new-product marketing at a mid-sized firm in West Paris, Maine, that manufactures safety equipment. Your firm recently designed and began producing a new type of plastic safety goggles. A special coating, applied during the manufacturing process, radically minimizes the possibility of the goggles' fogging up on the inside. (Assume that fogging is a common problem in safety goggles, because of perspiration and because of many manufacturing conditions in which goggles are used.) Your firm wants you to market the new goggles to a large manufacturer of lawn mowers that has several plants throughout New England. Your contact is Ms. Sharon Shapiro, vice president of manufacturing at Lawn Helper Products of Hartford, Connecticut.

Using this fictitious case, and inventing additional details when necessary, report on how you would work through the twelve-step sales proposal process outlined in this chapter. Be specific about your objectives and techniques at each step of the process.

3. *In-house proposal process: Real content*

(This exercise can serve as the basis for a discussion, oral report, or written report.)

For the context of this exercise, use any organization to which you now belong—an employer, a civic group, or a college or university, for example. Select an idea that you could conceivably propose to the decision makers in this organization. Now report on how you would complete the five-step process for in-house proposals outlined in this chapter. Be specific about your objectives and techniques at each step of the process.

4. *In-house proposal process: Simulated content*

(This exercise can serve as the basis for a discussion, oral report, or written report.)

You are an engineer at a small firm that designs and installs heating, ventilating, and air-conditioning (HVAC) systems in new commercial buildings. You and 20 engineer colleagues write proposals for business, as well as project reports to your customers after each job is completed. Lately you seem to be spending about 75 percent of your time writing and polishing documents, taking too much time away from your technical work. Even then, you sometimes wonder about the quality of the final drafts. There's no in-house technical writer or editor, so it's up to the engineers and the word-processing operators to catch errors.

You are convinced that hiring a technical writer/editor would save the firm considerable money. Engineers would continue to write drafts, but the writer/editor could help by (1) suggesting organizational improvements, (2) making prose style clearer and more appropriate for readers, and (3) working with the operators to eliminate mechanical and grammatical errors.

Your major obstacle is the strong opinion of the manager of engineering: you have heard him declare that all engineers should be expert writers and, therefore, responsible for their own reports and proposals. Given this obstacle, report on how you would complete this chapter's five-step process for in-house proposals. Be specific about your objectives and techniques at each step of the process.

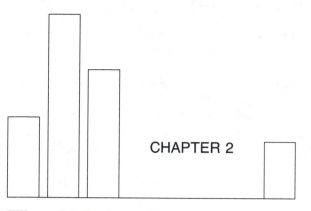

CHAPTER 2

The Writing Process

OBJECTIVES

- ○ Survey the three writing stages of planning, drafting, and editing
- ○ Anticipate obstacles your readers face
- ○ Learn steps for determining your readers' needs
- ○ Learn to write effective outlines
- ○ Distinguish the term *format* from *organization*
- ○ Find ways to overcome "writer's block"
- ○ Learn the Main Principle of Organization and some related organization rules
- ○ Learn the general steps of the editing process
- ○ Understand the team-writing process of storyboarding

Writing a successful proposal is a process. Good writers know that their rigor in completing this series of steps determines the quality of the final product, whether a proposal, letter, memorandum, report, or other document. You should spend about equal amounts of time on these three main steps in the writing process:

1. Planning your approach
2. Producing early drafts
3. Editing final drafts

This chapter mainly concerns the first stage, the planning process. But we will also look briefly at the other two stages, producing and editing drafts.

Details about drafting and editing will be covered in Parts Two and Three.

For those new to business and technical writing, this chapter offers enough information to get you started on a writing project. For veterans of on-the-job writing, it provides a refresher course in the writing process. Most of the chapter describes the tasks of an *individual* writer. The "Storyboarding" section, however, describes a *team-writing* approach to writing proposals.

Learning About the Reader

The planning stage of writing requires you to answer a most important question: Exactly what do your readers want to read? To answer that question, we will examine obstacles most readers face, and then outline strategies you can use to listen better to your readers and analyze their needs.

Obstacles Readers Face. For the moment, forget about your problems as a writer and consider instead the readers' difficulties. Most letter and proposal readers share four concerns.

Obstacle #1: They are impatient.

Readers are easily frustrated. No matter how complex the document, they want to get quickly to the heart of it. Some observers suggest that readers' impatience and anxiety have increased dramatically in the last few decades. Shorter attention spans and an overzealous interest in "time management" are two of the culprits blamed for changing the way people read. Whether you bemoan or relish this new "I want it now" reading habit, your writing should take it into account.

Obstacle #2: They are busy.

Readers won't have time to move through your proposal without interruption. Their concentration will be broken by constant phone calls, meetings, and emergencies. If your proposal isn't written so that it's easy to get back into, it won't get much attention.

Obstacle #3: They lack knowledge of your field and/or your product.

Readers probably don't have your knowledge of the proposal topic; that's why *you* are writing the proposal. When in doubt about what readers know, it's best to assume they know very little and provide the necessary background. Few, if any, readers will begrudge you the space for this background information. Those who don't need it can always skip to another part of the proposal.

Obstacle #4: They share decision-making authority with others, who may have different backgrounds and interests.

You rarely have the luxury of writing to only one reader. Instead, your proposal will usually be evaluated by a number of people with varied interests. Therefore, even if several key readers favor your proposal, they are often in the position of having to convince others with different needs and interests. Your job is to develop a strategy for overcoming these obstacles. Polishing your listening skills should be your first step.

Features of a Good Listener. People love to discuss their problems—much more than they want you to give easy solutions. In fact, most clients and managers are almost begging for someone to listen to their travails. Before they will see you as the right person to help them out, you must first show an interest in understanding their concerns. Specifically, how can you demonstrate this interest?

- By spending most of your time asking questions in early conversations with the client or manager, rather than talking about what you have to offer.
- By showing patience in listening to responses, even when conversations depart from the immediate subject at hand. (After all, you may discover additional needs to which you can respond in later proposals.)
- By taking careful notes, both to demonstrate the importance you place on their comments and to retrieve information to use later in writing the proposal.

Let's say, for example, that you are convinced your firm should develop a "satellite" word-processing system. The system could comprise small centers on each of the five floors in company headquarters, replacing the present centralized system on the third floor. Believing that the change will meet the company's needs and will encounter no resistance, you're anxious to write the proposal to your manager. Before writing, however, it would be a good idea to meet with your manager and any other supervisors who would be affected by the proposed change, for these two reasons:

1. To give them the opportunity to vent their frustrations about the inefficiencies of the present one-floor system (like you, they are tired of dropping off and picking up documents many times each day)

2. To get them to buy into the idea behind your proposal even before you write it

In short, focus on getting to know the decision makers by asking questions and taking good notes.

There is a further benefit of careful listening during these preproposal conversations. Often the potential reader will drop hints about points you should address in the proposal and the format that would be most appropriate. Before you even begin to write, you may find that questions like these have already been answered for you:

- ○ What features of the idea should be stressed?
- ○ How important is the project schedule?
- ○ Who should be involved in the work?
- ○ How many product or service options should be presented?
- ○ Is a formal or informal proposal format appropriate?
- ○ How long should the proposal be?

By doing your homework—that is, by *really* listening to those whose problems you wish to solve—you stand the best chance of writing a responsive, successful proposal.

Analyzing Reader Needs. After preproposal meetings, you need to analyze the readers' needs before you write even the first line. A thorough analysis will yield information you can use to design the document itself.

Reader Analysis Step #1: Write down what you know about your readers.

Don't trust your memory to retain all the important details about your audience. Force yourself to record answers to these questions:

1. What do they want from your proposal?
2. What actions do you want them to take?
3. What role do they have in their organization?
4. What features of their professional training could affect their reading of the proposal?
5. What features of their personal backgrounds or lifestyles could affect their response to the proposal?

Don't be upset if you aren't able to fill a sheet of paper with what you know. If the questions were easy to answer, more proposal writers would ask them rather than ignore them. At this stage, it's just as important to find out what you *don't* know.

Reader Analysis Step #2: Talk with colleagues who may have written a proposal to the same person.

Your colleagues are often eager to share their knowledge of someone's needs. For external sales proposals, check company files to find out who may have written to the same client. You may discover that someone has prepared a similar proposal to the readers you're now addressing; visit that person's office or take him or her to lunch. A little low-key research of this sort will give you lots of data that might not surface otherwise.

For in-house proposals, it is easier to get inside information about potential readers.

- Question those who work for the reader
- Read proposals the readers have previously accepted
- Look into the readers' background—education, years with the firm, pet projects, etc.

Reader Analysis Step #3: Pinpoint the decision maker(s) in your audience.

The decision makers' needs should be uppermost in your mind as you begin to outline and then to write your document. As we will discuss later in the chapter, you particularly need to direct the beginning and end of your proposal to readers who will make decisions based on what you write.

Reader Analysis Step #4: When, despite your efforts, reader information is hard to come by, keep the proposal as simple as possible.

For most of us, learning to write is a process of unlearning much of what we learned in school about sounding "educated." When in doubt, keep it simple—short words, short sentences, well-defined terms, and lots of headings and lists. The following suggestions for writing an outline will help you maintain simplicity and clarity and achieve solid organization.

Writing Outlines

Information gathered from the analysis of your readers' needs will form the basis for your proposal outline. Outlining helps you organize the information. To some, the word *outline* harks back to junior-high English assignments that required flawless alignment of Roman numerals and careful subordination. Discard this notion; outlines don't have to be pretty, just functional. Follow these steps to write outlines that will lead to well-organized first drafts. (The "Storyboarding" section later in this chapter describes a team-writing approach to outlines.)

Outline Step #1: Brainstorm on the subject of your proposal.

Jot down all the ideas that enter your head about the proposal's content. Specifically, focus on the problem your proposal addresses and the solution you propose. At this stage don't concern yourself with wording, redundancy, sequence of ideas, or other fine points. Also, develop only the ideas for the body of the proposal. Save the beginning and ending sections until later; they are easier to outline and write after you have dealt with the proposal proper.

Outline Step #2: Distinguish major ideas from minor ones, deleting weak or redundant points.

Here is a four-step process for imposing order on a page of unorganized notes created during Outline Step #1:

1. Circle the three to seven main points that will serve as basic building blocks of the proposal (experts suggest that readers best remember points grouped in three to seven units).

2. Connect subordinate points with arrows to the main points they support.

3. Delete redundant or weak points.

4. Number the circled main points according to their anticipated sequence in the proposal.

If your paper is a mess, you're doing it right! The point is that a working outline is rarely neat. You must wrest form from chaos!

Outline Step #3: Rewrite the outline.

To write your draft, you'll probably need a neater outline than the scribbled sheet resulting from Outline Step #2. In your rewrite, you should

- Place points in the order they will appear in your draft
- Cluster minor points below their respective major points
- Show relationships with dashes, indention, underlining, the familiar Roman numeral system, or any other arrangement that works for you
- Put all points either in topic or sentence form

Concerning the last point, topic form is preferable. Topic outlines comprise fragmented ideas rather than sentences—for example, "Ten previous projects at site" as opposed to "Our firm has completed ten previous projects at the site." These outlines are concise and less likely than sentence outlines to lock you in too early to specific, and perhaps undesirable, phrasing. Also, they are well suited to the team-writing process of storyboarding we will discuss later.

Outline Step #4: Check the outline for development and clarity.

As this stage, again evaluate how well you have developed the outline. Further expand upon an idea if its support appears weak. Any point that is subdivided will, of course, always have at least two subordinate points.

Outline Step #5: Don't follow this "final" outline too rigidly.

An outline is meant to be fluid, organic—it will necessarily change as you begin the always creative and therefore unpredictable process of writing a draft.

Choosing Formats

Format is different from organization. *Organization* refers to the arrangement of information within sentences, paragraphs, sections, and entire documents. Your outline helped you struggle with organization; and, in the drafting process, you will struggle with it further. Since readers have little patience with poorly organized letters and proposals, organization is crucial. Unlike organization, however, *format* is more a matter of mechanics and thus concerns questions like these:

- Is a memorandum proposal or a formal proposal better?
- Should the cover letter be bound with the proposal?
- Should graphics appear in the text or in appendices?
- What is the appropriate type of heading system?

Sometimes you will have few difficult decisions about format because your company or the client has set guidelines. But if you do have the option of choosing a format for your letter or proposal, Chapters 3, 4, 5, 6, and 8 provide some criteria for selecting a format.

Writing Drafts

After spending a lot of time in the planning stage, you are ready to start drafting. We use *drafting* to refer to the process of producing the text of your proposal, whether that text is handwritten or typed. Drafting does *not* include editing copy for style, grammar, or mechanics. If you're like most writers, you probably have two main concerns about writing a draft, particularly the first draft: you want to write as quickly as possible, and you want to be able to organize information appropriately.

Overcoming Writer's Block. Following three "fast draft" rules will help you start and then keep the words flowing.

Fast Draft Rule #1: Use an outline.

As mentioned, the outline keeps you on track while writing. It also gets you moving at the outset by listing details you can use as the content of your sentences.

Fast Draft Rule #2: Force yourself to write quickly.

Don't worry about errors in word choice, grammar, or mechanics; just get as much material onto paper as you can. Writers have problems when they dwell on every word, trying to create perfect copy during the drafting stage. Reserve that penchant for perfection for the editing process.

Fast Draft Rule #3: Begin with any section.

Don't feel compelled to write in the order the information occurs in the outline. Instead, start writing the body sections that you feel most inclined to write; then piece the draft together later. A good outline, of course, helps you skip from section to section during the drafting process.

Only after you have fleshed out all the body sections covered in the outline are you ready to write the parts of the proposal that are usually not outlined—the important beginning and ending sections like the summary, introduction, and conclusion. You can best write these overview sections *after* completing the body of the proposal.

Organizing Points for Busy Readers. Put bluntly, you must organize your draft with the assumption that it will be read carelessly. Usually, your readers:

- Are too busy to read entire documents
- Become bored with anything that runs more than a page or two
- Want to find information quickly
- Are continually interrupted
- Place the greatest importance on beginnings and endings

Though common to all readers, these qualities are shared especially by decision makers. Managers are too busy to read everything they receive. In fact, many have studied speed-reading techniques that stress skimming for key words. Whether requested or not, your proposal may more often be a target of cursory reading than other types of business writing. It is human nature to resist *any* sales message. Faced with these obstacles, what is a proposal writer to do? The answer can be framed in one simple principle of organization:

Put the Most Important Information First

This Main Principle of Organization should guide your entire drafting process from beginning to end. Here are four specific rules that will help you apply it.

Organization Rule #1: Define "important information" in terms of your readers.

Always consider the proposal from your readers' perspectives. People aren't interested in your product or service for itself; they're interested in what it will *do* for them.

Organization Rule #2: Put important information first in all units of the draft.

The Main Principle of Organization applies to individual paragraphs and sections just as to the entire draft.

- Each paragraph leads off with its overview (topic) sentence.
- Each section leads off with its overview paragraph or two.
- The proposal leads off with its overview section.

In other words, write every unit as if you're certain readers won't get beyond the first few sentences. They may not.

Organization Rule #3: Apply the Main Principle of Organization most rigorously to the first section.

You must provide in the first section a capsule version of everything you want the reader to remember. As we will see later, that section may be a paragraph in a short proposal or a page (at most!) in a long proposal. It will be this brief because it must be—there must be one section of the proposal to which the reader can turn for relief. This refreshing bit of brevity provides a change of pace from the thoroughness you have necessarily injected into the rest of your argument. If it pains you to condense your prose this way, remember this observation by theatrical producer David Belasco: "If you can't write your idea on the back of my calling card, then you don't have a clear idea."

Organization Rule #4: Make few exceptions to the Main Principle of Organization.

If you decide it's best *not* to place the main point first, be sure your readers will keep reading until they find it. For instance, you may decide that readers need to see your rationale for costs before you give them the actual numbers, so you lead up to the numbers rather than lead away from them. You will thus have prefaced the relatively high costs by an explanation of the unusual level of service your firm provides. There is, of course, a calculated risk in this technique. You're gambling that readers won't become irritated at being unable to find the exact cost easily, but at least you have a reason for breaking the Main Principle of Organization.

Editing

After you have written the draft, congratulate yourself on completing the hardest part of the process. Your burden was eased somewhat if you used the reader analysis sheets, a complete outline, the suggestions for overcoming writer's block, and the Main Principle of Organization. This strategy gives you organization and speed.

All is for naught, however, if you fail to edit well in the important final stage of writing. Because Chapter 8 lists specific guidelines, we will list here only the three main steps in the editing process. You should complete each step for every document you write.

Editing Step #1: Refine style.

Your first pass at editing a draft should focus on a variety of stylistic matters; for example, you should

- Carefully consider individual word choices
- Vary sentence length and structure
- Check the coherence of paragraphs
- Make sure all units conform to the Main Principle of Organization
- Add useful typographical features (like the bullets used in this list)
- Make sure all graphics are referred to accurately in the text

In short, editing for style allows you to make the changes that will entice people to read the document, rather than just giving them the information they need. This type of editing, moreover, gives a letter or proposal your individual stamp. Each person's writing style is quite personal, even unique, and it is every bit as important a tool in swaying the reader as is content. View style as a flexible device that you can adjust to meet different needs of different readers. Remember—you are writing for your reader, not yourself.

Editing Step #2: Correct grammar.

Grammar is the downfall of many writers. People in all fields consider grammatical accuracy a reflection of the writer's overall professionalism and intelligence. When they see problems with grammatical errors, they often respond by

- Searching for additional errors
- Paying less attention to content
- Doubting the writer's ability to do the work set forth in the proposal

Your readers may not respond this strongly, but you can never be certain. You would be wise to strive for correctness.

Editing Step #3: Proofread for mechanical errors.

Remember that the responsibility for documents you sign rests with you, not with a secretary or company proofreader. Always give your letter or proposal a final check for errors like these:

- Misspellings
- Misplaced pages
- Incorrect page numbers
- Missing lines of text
- Missing appendices
- Errors in cost figures

Chapter 8 suggests a process for avoiding all such errors. It is worth noting here, however, that the best proofreaders are those who also rely on the proofing skills of colleagues. Many professionals adopt a "buddy system" whereby two people help each other proofread documents they have written individually. Another set of eyes sometimes does wonders.

Storyboarding

So far in this chapter we have examined the writing process you complete individually. Sometimes, however, you will be asked to work on proposals with a team of your colleagues. Many firms now use a technique called *storyboarding* to plan and write group proposals.

Definition. Proposal storyboarding derives from a technique first used in Hollywood for writing movie scripts. The process requires you to outline your ideas in two-page units or storyboards. As the sample board in Figure 2-1 shows, a storyboard usually includes five parts:

1. Information that identifies the proposal
2. A statement of the storyboard's topic
3. A summary sentence for the entire storyboard
4. Key sentences for developing paragraphs later in the draft
5. A rough sketch of one complementary visual

When all the storyboards for a proposal have been completed, you and your writing team meet to evaluate each other's boards. Each revised storyboard then becomes the basis for a two-page module within the proposal draft. We assume that two pages of draft contain about 750 words with a half-page visual, or 500 words with a full-page visual.

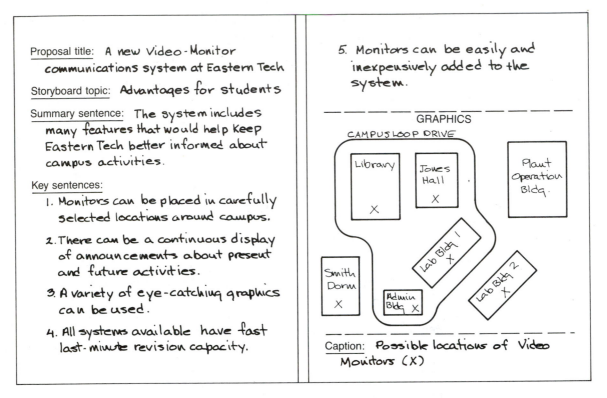

Proposal title: A new Video-Monitor communications system at Eastern Tech

Storyboard topic: Advantages for students

Summary sentence: The system includes many features that would help keep Eastern Tech better informed about campus activities.

Key sentences:

1. Monitors can be placed in carefully selected locations around campus.

2. There can be a continuous display of announcements about present and future activities.

3. A variety of eye-catching graphics can be used.

4. All systems available have fast last-minute revision capacity.

5. Monitors can be easily and inexpensively added to the system.

GRAPHICS

CAMPUS LOOP DRIVE

Library X

Jones Hall X

Plant Operation Bldg.

Lab Bldg 1 X

Smith Dorm X

Admin Bldg X

Lab Bldg 2 X

Caption: Possible locations of Video Monitors (X)

FIGURE 2–1 Sample Storyboard

Storyboarding greatly affects both the product and process of your writing. Concerning product, your proposal becomes a narrative or story composed of many relatively short, strung-together units. Each unit has an accompanying visual aid to reinforce the unit's topic. Concerning process, you receive thorough peer evaluations at the outline stage of writing, not at the drafting stage. These storyboard sessions also permit you to see how your part of the project meshes with those of other writers.

Procedure.   As shown in Figure 2-2, storyboarding involves a rigorous procedure. Though it requires the joint efforts of everyone on the team, it should be overseen by one person. This manager/editor must constantly work to focus the efforts of many toward achieving one goal. Without such structure, the process may degenerate into the kind of time-wasting free-for-all that characterizes so many team-writing efforts.

The seven steps that follow apply best to large, solicited (requested) sales proposals. With a little modification, however, the procedure can work for in-house proposals as well as unsolicited (unrequested) sales proposals.

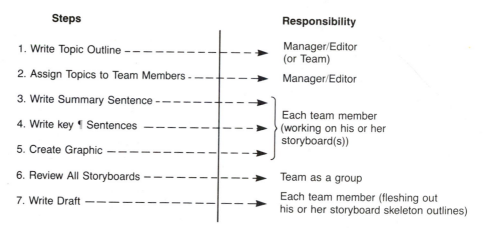

FIGURE 2–2   Storyboard Process: Seven Steps

Storyboard Step #1: Write a topic outline for the proposal.

The outline, prepared by the manager/editor or by the whole group, must include all the storyboard topics. Each topic on the outline becomes the material for a separate board. As we noted when we discussed outlines, a "topic" on a topic outline is an idea in fragment rather than sentence form; for example, "fewer quality control problems" would belong on a topic outline, whereas "The ABC system will create fewer quality control problems" would not.

In solicited sales proposals, your topics will probably come directly from a close reading of the written request for proposal or RFP (Chapter 4 presents an RFP example). In unsolicited sales proposals and all in-house proposals, your topic outline will arise from careful scrutiny of the readers' needs and your proposed response to these needs. Whatever the case, the success of the storyboard process rests on the clarity and substance of the topic outline.

Storyboard Step #2: Assign topics to appropriate members of the proposal team.

Storyboarding involves individual as well as group work. The proposal manager/editor assigns topics to those who are best equipped to develop them; then the individual team members work on their own to write the storyboards for which they are responsible.

Storyboard Step #3: Write a clear, comprehensive summary sentence for the storyboard.

With your storyboard assignment in hand, first write a summary sentence that provides an umbrella for all details. Much like the thesis sentence for an essay, it gives you direction for writing the storyboard's text and visual. (You may want to refine this summary sentence after you have completed Steps 4 and 5.)

Storyboard Step #4: Write key sentences for each main paragraph.

These sentences, usually three to seven per board, become the topic sentences for each of your main paragraphs in the text. Make sure each key sentence has the potential to be developed into a solid paragraph.

It does not follow, however, that all paragraphs from the text will have a corresponding key sentence on a storyboard. Some paragraphs, particularly shorter ones, serve as introductory or transitional devices within the proposal.

Storyboard Step #5: Create an appropriate graphic for each storyboard.

Storyboarding obviously relies heavily on graphics in that each board includes one. Every main idea—that is, every storyboard topic—must use a graphic to reinforce some point in the board's text. The theory behind this procedure is that text and graphics should work together, in complementary fashion, to drive home each point. The storyboard itself need include only a rough sketch of the table or figure you plan to use, which you can later refine. (Chapter 7 contains guidelines for seven common types of proposal graphics.)

Storyboard Step #6: Review all storyboards in meeting(s) with your proposal team.

Here's how these evaluation sessions work:

- All storyboards are attached to the walls in sequence, so that participants can see the skeleton for the entire proposal.
- The proposal manager/editor leads the discussion by denoting the summary sentence, key points, and visual for each storyboard.
- Team members offer suggestions on each storyboard and, ideally, reach a consensus on each one.

Storyboard Step #7: Use the revised storyboards to create a draft that includes graphics.

After the team has critiqued the storyboards, the process reverts to individual efforts. Using the revised boards, you write the draft sections for which you have produced storyboards. When all the draft sections have been written, the proposal manager/editor usually assumes the task of assembling the entire proposal package.

Benefits and Drawbacks. The main benefit of storyboarding is that it makes group work flow smoothly. Team members find it easier to grasp and then comment upon simple outlined points than to evaluate complete text. Writers are also less likely to react defensively to criticism when they have written only outlines rather than entire drafts. Besides allowing groups to function better, the storyboard technique has these additional benefits:

○ Drafts undergo fewer revisions, since they flow from an agreed-upon outline.

○ Visuals are solidly incorporated into the body of the proposal rather than added as afterthoughts.

○ The reader receives information in manageable, two-page chunks.

There are, however, a few drawbacks to storyboarding. First, the system takes real planning and coordination. All the firm's proposal writers must be trained to use the process *before* they are asked to follow it for an actual proposal, and the group should take no shortcuts in the seven-stage procedure, no matter how frenzied the proposal-writing situation. Second, some proposal writers may have to rearrange their thinking about the use of visuals. Third, the process requires strong managers/editors, with excellent writing *and* interpersonal skills, to coordinate the efforts of diverse team members. For the firm willing to face these challenges, storyboarding can create team-written proposals that win.

SUMMARY

Successful writing results from careful attention to the three-stage process of planning, drafting, and editing. This chapter has examined a series of steps and writing rules to help you complete this process.

Most proposal readers face these four obstacles: they are impatient, very busy, not familiar with what you are proposing, and not the exclusive decision makers. To reach these harried readers, you must first become a good listener by asking questions, listening patiently to responses, and taking notes. You can further analyze and respond to the readers' needs by:

1. Writing down what you know about them
2. Talking with others who have written for the same readers
3. Pinpointing the decision maker(s)
4. Keeping the proposal as simple as possible

With information in hand about your readers, next construct a practical outline. Write down all the points you want to develop, distinguish major ideas from minor ones, delete weak or redundant points, give the outline a final check for development, and change the outline when necessary during the writing process.

Writing the first draft is your next step. You can overcome writer's block by using your outline religiously, forcing yourself to write quickly, and beginning with whatever section you feel most inspired to write. In every section, however, follow the Main Principle of Organization: put the most important information first.

Editing completes the writing cycle. At the editing stage you refine style, correct grammar, and proofread carefully.

When writing a proposal with others, the writing process becomes more efficient with storyboarding, involving these seven steps:

1. Writing a topic outline for the proposal
2. Assigning topics to appropriate members of the proposal team
3. Writing a clear, comprehensive summary sentence for the storyboard
4. Writing key sentences for each main paragraph
5. Creating an appropriate graphic for each storyboard
6. Reviewing all storyboards in meeting(s) with your proposal team
7. Using the revised storyboards to create a draft that includes graphics

EXERCISES

1. *Analyzing reader needs: In-house proposal*

   (This exercise can serve as a basis for a discussion, oral report, or written report.)

   For this exercise, use any organization to which you now belong—for example, your employer, a civic group, or your college or university. Select an idea that you could conceivably propose as a member of that organization. Now report on how you would follow the steps outlined in this chapter for determining the needs of your readers.

2. *Analyzing reader needs: Sales proposal*

   (This exercise can serve as the basis for a discussion, oral report, or written report.)

Use company data from your own or others' work experience. Assume that you want to market a product, service, or idea to a new or to a familiar client. Now report on how you would follow the steps outlined in this chapter for determining your readers' needs.

3. *Preparing an outline: Your experience*

Assume that you are preparing to write either an in-house or sales proposal. (Use the context described in Exercise #1 or #2 above.) Follow the five-step process described in this chapter to create an outline to guide your draft.

4. *Preparing an outline: Simulation*

Assume that you are one of twenty project managers for a 500-employee firm that builds small shopping centers in the Midwest. Besides the main office in St. Louis, where you work, there are smaller offices in St. Paul, Chicago, Dayton, Fort Wayne, Topeka, and Dubuque. Until now, the company has survived without an in-house safety engineer. Increased business and liability, however, have convinced you to propose hiring a full-time safety engineer.

You have first determined that your main proposal readers would be the vice-president for engineering, vice-president for finance, and personnel director. After analyzing their needs, you completed Outline Step #1—that is, you brainstormed and wrote down all the major and minor points your proposal should include, in no particular order. (The result is the jumbled list below.) Using this list as your starting point, complete Outline Steps #2, distinguishing major from minor points, and #3, eliminating redundant or weak items. Then rewrite the outline by (1) showing some points as subpoints of others, (2) putting ideas in their proper sequence, and (3) placing all points in topic form. In this case, place what you consider the most important information first in the rewritten outline.

_____ Cited by Occupational Health and Safety Administration (OSHA) for ten safety violations last year

_____ One three-day job shutdown by OSHA

_____ Workers often don't wear hard hats or other safety gear

_____ Safety training has been infrequent

_____ Most new employees learn what little they do know on the job, not from training

_____ Uneven quality in the courses given by the few outside consultants that have been used

_____ Exit interviews with employees leaving the firm indicate on-the-job safety is one of the main reasons for leaving

_____ Equipment insurance costs escalated 15 percent last year—agent says that two-thirds of that increase was due to excessive accidents

_____ Safety engineer can do training at all offices

_____ Morale will improve at all levels when employees see firm's safety commitment

_____ Hazardous wastes have been found on some construction sites—no one knows how to detect or handle them

_____ Some large clients have expressed surprise that the company does not have a safety specialist

_____ Joe Nunn, the engineer with the best safety background, is spread thin trying to act as a safety engineer (which he is not) and doing his main job—supervising construction projects

_____ Office workers could benefit from preventive programs on smoking, alcohol, drug abuse, etc.

_____ Need someone who can talk the same language as the insurance agents and OSHA

_____ Can hire good safety engineer for about $35,000 (about the same as construction engineers with a few years of experience)

_____ Safety engineer could train, observe projects, negotiate insurance rates, etc.

5. *Organizing information: Simulation*

Use the Main Principle of Organization to rewrite this paragraph:

When our firm was founded ten years ago, there were just two secretaries—Mary Watts and Jim Jamison—to handle all the typing and filing responsibilities for fifteen consulting engineers. With their heavy workload, they needed to resolve questions quickly about the format of documents and office filing procedures. With no official manual available, they simply discussed problems as they encountered them. Frequent communication was the key. Now, however, we have twelve secretaries handling the workload of over one hundred engineers in a four-story building. Without the opportunity to meet frequently, these secretaries often end up using different standards. Clearly, we need a document procedures manual to eliminate this confusion.

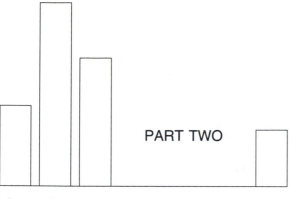

PART TWO

GUIDELINES AND MODELS FOR WRITING

In Chapter 1, we placed proposal writing into the larger context of building long-term relationships with clients and managers. Chapter 2 outlined the planning, drafting, and editing stages of writing, with emphasis on planning. Chapters 3, 4, 5, and 6 will help you meet the challenge of writing these documents of persuasion:

○ Sales letters (Chapter 3)
○ Formal sales proposals (Chapter 4)
○ Informal sales proposals (Chapter 5)
○ In-house proposals (Chapter 6)

We will define some important terms you will encounter in these chapters and in the professional world in the form of answers to five central questions about sales letter and proposal writing.

Question #1: Is your preproposal correspondence external or internal?

Sales Letters. The term *sales letter* as used in this book refers to proposal-related correspondence with someone in another organization. Because these letters strengthen relationships, they increase the likelihood of getting work both now and later.

Sales Memos. Within the same organization, sales correspondence is called a *sales memo.* Although you usually communicate in person with these readers, memos occasionally precede or follow an in-house proposal.

Question #2: Has the proposal been requested?

Unsolicited Proposals. If you submit a proposal without a request from a would-be reader, the proposal is *unsolicited.*

Solicited Proposals. If the proposal is requested, it is *solicited.* The request to submit a proposal may come informally (by phone or in conversation), or it may come through a formal written request, a *request for proposal* (RFP). You should follow explicitly whatever guidelines the client lists in an RFP.

Question #3: Is the proposal to a client or to your boss?

External Proposals. If you direct a proposal to someone in another organization, the proposal is *external*, for it will be evaluated by people outside your organization.

In-house Proposals. If you write a proposal to someone within your own firm, the proposal is termed *in-house* or *internal*. Some in-house proposals can have features of external proposals. If you work as a geologist for a large oil company, for example, your in-house proposal to purchase new equipment may be evaluated by a company division quite separate and distant from yours. In that case, you would face some of the challenges encountered when writing to someone in another organization.

Question #4: What are you selling?

Sales Proposals. If your external proposal promotes a product, service, or idea, it is a *sales proposal*—the most important form of external proposal used in business and industry.

Grant or R & D Proposals. If your external proposal seeks funding to perform research or to develop a product, it is a *grant* or *research and development* (R & D) proposal. Occasionally, an R & D proposal can be internal if writers seek funding for research within their own organization. Each funding agency tends to develop its own proposal guidelines, which you should follow scrupulously. Although

we will not specifically cover grant proposals, many of the basic guidelines in this book apply to them.

Planning Proposals. A request for support for an internal change in procedures is termed a *planning proposal*. Such a document is almost always internal, as in the case of an accountant's proposing adoption of a new approach to filing accounts-payable forms.

Question #5: What format is most appropriate?

Informal Proposals. Short, less complex proposals are usually presented in an *informal format*. If done "in house," they are often in memorandum format and may be called *memo proposals*. They lack formalities such as binding, cover page, or table of contents. Memo proposals also lead off in typical memorandum style with Date/To/From/Subject lines.

Informal proposals written to someone outside your organization are usually in letter form and may thus be called *letter proposals*. Although letter proposals can be as long as five pages of text, excluding attachments, most are just a few pages.

Formal Proposals. Whether internal or external, most proposals that are more than five pages long adopt the rigid format of a *formal proposal*, complete with a cover, table of contents, and a host of other major sections. Lengthy formal proposals are often in several volumes.

Several cautions and reminders must accompany such a prescriptive set of definitions.

- As noted, these terms overlap considerably.
- The terms provide convenient handles, but are not definitions to be etched in

stone. Companies for which you complete work may use other terms, so be ready to adopt your readers' terminology and formats.

○ This text describes only the most common form of sales correspondence, *sales letters*. Sales memos are used much less frequently, since you usually have the opportunity to meet in person with in-house readers of your proposals.

○ This text deals only with the two most common types of proposals in business and industry: internal planning (here called simply *in-house*) and external sales (here called simply *sales*).

○ Proposals of all types have essentially the same persuasive goals. Whether the decision makers are managers in your own firm or clients in another, these readers must become convinced that you can fulfill their needs.

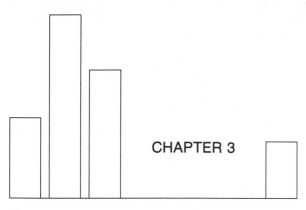

CHAPTER 3

Sales Letters

OBJECTIVES
- ○ Learn the general reasons for writing sales letters
- ○ Discover specific opportunities for writing sales letters during the proposal process
- ○ Learn the writing rules that apply to most sales letters
- ○ Examine model sales letters (with marginal comments and summary critiques)
- ○ Practice letter-writing exercises using the chapter's guidelines

In the context of this book, sales letters comprise all correspondence that relates to your proposal. We are *not* describing the direct-mail letters of the type that you receive in your home mail.

Chapter 1 stressed the importance of contacting the prospective client many times, both in person and in writing. As one method of contact, the sales letter gives you a tremendous opportunity to influence your reader. To help you write powerful letters, this chapter includes background information, writing rules, models, and exercises.

Why and When to Write Sales Letters

Many writers view the sales proposal as a stand-alone document that will succeed or fail on its own merits. In fact, it depends heavily on all the client contacts that precede it. There are three main reasons for making sales letters an important part of your preproposal work.

Reason #1: To reinforce

Letters help to reinforce and clarify what is discussed in person. You can use them to summarize a discussion, provide a formal record of points discussed, and highlight important issues.

Reason #2: To follow up

Letters give you the opportunity to respond to questions that you may not have been able to answer during a meeting. You can also provide additional material (brochures, specs, flyers, articles) that you think will help clients. They will appreciate this kind of follow up, particularly since so few people provide it.

Reason #3: To exercise control

Letters help you maintain the initiative, to retain control. They remind clients that you're still there, ready to do whatever necessary to meet their needs. In other words, they keep you in control of the proposal process.

Chapter 1 mentioned some points at which letters can be written in the context of the cycle of contacts with the client. These letter-writing opportunities are worth reviewing before we move on to guidelines for format and content. Letters can be used to:

1. Start a relationship ("I'll be calling you . . .")
2. Follow up a phone call ("good talking to you . . . can we meet next week to discuss your needs regarding . . .")
3. Follow up a meeting ("you mentioned that you could use more information on . . . so here's an article that might interest you . . .")
4. Provide a strong lead-off to a formal proposal ("the major benefit this proposal offers you is . . .")
5. Follow up acceptance of your proposal ("you've chosen the firm that will pay close attention to your need for quality work . . .")
6. Follow up rejection of your proposal ("we learned a great deal about your firm and hope to do business with you another time . . . is there some way our proposal could have been made more responsive to your needs?")

7. Cushion the blow of the invoice ("we have appreciated your business and will call next week to see if you have any further follow-up questions . . .")

8. Seek repeat business ("we enjoyed working with you last October . . . we now offer a new product that might interest you . . .")

Ten Rules for Writing Sales Letters

Some people seem to have a flair for writing, just as some people seem to be "born" salespeople. Writing good letters, however, is much more a matter of applying basic communication strategies than it is an innate gift. You can *develop* competence in letter writing, as in sales, by learning some fundamentals and then putting them into action. (And, you'll find that writing letters gets easier the more often you do it.)

As always, the key is to discover just what the reader wants from the letter. Indeed, here is the underlying question that occupies all readers' minds as they approach your letter: "What's in this for me?" You can respond best to readers' needs by writing a visually appealing letter and by making important information easy to find. The ten guidelines that follow speak to issues of both format and content. As you begin to use them, you will see that an effective letter becomes a powerful tool in your effort to satisfy customers.

Letter Rule #1: Use the diamond-shaped rhetorical pattern.

Readers are most likely to give attention to "easy-in, easy-out" letters—that is, those that are easy to begin reading and easy to exit. Figure 3-1 shows a visual pattern for sales letters that responds to this reader need. Short first and last paragraphs give readers the quick impression that they can read your letter in a minute or less. If the format immediately creates this feeling of comfort, your message will then get maximum attention.

Letter Rule #2: Use the 3-Cs pattern to gain and keep reader interest.

You can gain and keep the reader's interest by following this simple three-part guideline—the 3 Cs:

1. *Capture* interest with a good opener.
2. *Convince* with powerful supporting points.
3. *Control* response by making clear the next step.

Even if readers have already expressed interest in what you're selling, don't be lulled into thinking they will anxiously await your letter. Because

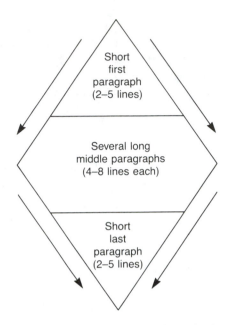

FIGURE 3-1 Diamond Pattern for Sales Letters

reading *any* document is a chore for most busy people, use the 3-Cs pattern to entice readers to start the letter and keep them reading. Here are specific techniques to satisfy the 3-Cs pattern.

Letter Rule #3: Capture interest with a strong first paragraph.

Readers are most receptive at the start of a letter—they want to know *who* you are and *how* your letter can help them. So you need to capture their attention in the first paragraph by (1) showing that what you have to say will help solve a problem, and (2) providing some reference or link to your last contact with the reader. Successful first paragraphs respond to the reader who is thinking, "What does this letter have to do with me? And how can it help solve my problem?" These are ten techniques for attracting the reader's interest.

1. Cite a surprising fact
2. Announce a new service or product
3. Ask a question
4. Show understanding of the client's problem
5. Show potential for solving the client's problem
6. Present a testimonial
7. Make a challenging claim

8. Summarize results of the meeting
9. Present a "what/if" scenario
10. Answer a question the reader has previously asked

A good opening paragraph uses a combination of the first and second items. A poor opening paragraph squanders an opportunity to capture interest. These are examples of a good and a poor opening paragraph:

> I enjoyed meeting with you yesterday and learning about your product lines. You noted that Lathe #7 has a bearing problem. Have you considered solving the problem with a change out? Here's how it might work.

> Pursuant to your request for more information on our new-generation ball bearing product, I have enclosed a recent brochure. We believe this product offers state-of-the-art technology, and it is the pride of our firm.

The second example is, of course, the poor one, because it relies on old-fashioned, stilted business jargon like "pursuant to." It also focuses almost exclusively on the writer's view of his product, rather than the reader's concern about the bearing problem. A sales letter is no time to brag. Instead, it should approach the problem from the reader's perspective, even to the point of using pronouns like "you" rather than "I" and "we." The good example includes more natural language and an unobtrusive reference to the meeting the previous day. Most important, it focuses on the client's problem and then suggests a way to solve it. The question ("Have you considered . . .") encourages the reader to continue.

Letter Rule #4: Convince your readers in the body paragraphs.

After gaining your reader's attention, you must follow through on whatever promise the first paragraph held. Here are some guidelines for writing the body paragraphs:

- See every point from the readers' perspectives. Word every sentence to attract their interest. That's the only way to keep clients reading past the first paragraph.
- Use a deductive (general-to-specific) plan of organization in each paragraph. This means your first sentence—often the topic sentence—should state the point most important to the reader. The remaining sentences should support the first one. Unfortunately, too many writers bury main points in the middle of paragraphs or lead up to them at the end. Failing to include the main point in the first sentence assumes that readers have time to discover your purpose. They don't. Fast readers often focus on first sentences. If your paragraph does not start with an important idea, some people may skip the paragraph altogether.

○ Use the client's name in the body of the letter. Leading off a paragraph with a sentence like "Ms. Janowsky, you mentioned that you wanted to modernize your filing system" gives the personal touch that helps build relationships. Whether you use the first or last name depends, of course, on how you address someone in person.

○ Stress one main selling point throughout the letter. The body of a letter from a service firm, for example, should leave the reader with *one* image of that company—its quality work, service after the sale, or leadership in research and development. Avoid the "shotgun" approach, whereby you blast the reader with a long list of attributes.

○ Work from what they need to what you have to offer. Once you have established need, there is a better chance that the reader will be receptive to any talk about what you have to offer.

○ Emphasize what is unique about your firm or idea. Your best selling point is usually that which separates you from your competitors.

○ Explain the value of enclosures. Items like brochures and specification sheets won't get the attention they deserve if you don't mention their value. Enclosures have to be *sold*, not just sent. Also, if your letter gets separated from the enclosures (as often happens), you want the letter text to have been clear about the importance of what you sent.

○ Link value with price, if price needs to be mentioned at all. You don't have to be defensive about what your product, service, or idea will cost—*if* the client clearly sees the value. Also, don't put a lot of dollar figures in paragraph form. Numbers will be hard to find and will therefore tend to make readers suspicious of your prices. Instead, put prices in lists or tables, either within the letter or on enclosures.

Letter Rule #5: Control the next move with your last paragraph.

Just as the first paragraph gives you a great opportunity, so does the last one. This short paragraph is easy to write if you follow one main guideline: leave yourself, not the reader, in control of the next step. That usually means you should conclude with comments like these:

"I'll give you a call within a few days to arrange an appointment time that's convenient for you."

"The proposal will be in the mail next week."

"Bob and I are looking forward to the meeting scheduled for next week."

Unless you're in the enviable position of having clients clamoring at your door, they don't have much reason to call you after they receive a letter. Even if they do decide to call, you would not control the timing. Thus the reference to a follow-up call is an excellent way to end most letters. Just make sure you keep a reminder file so that you actually *make* all those promised calls!

Letter Rule #6: Break up body paragraphs for easy reading.

Here are a few of the most useful devices for organizing information into chunks:

- Numbered points
- Bulleted points (like those in this list)
- Subheadings

When using any of these structural devices, try to develop points in groups of *three.* Such groupings create a certain rhythm, attract attention, and encourage recall. Also, a short listing is more appropriate for a short document with a brief message, like a letter.

Letter Rule #7: Add a postscript for special attention.

The success of most letters depends only on having the first paragraph capture interest, the middle paragraphs convince the reader, and the last paragraph control the outcome. But occasionally you will have something else to say—a special offer, a reminder about a meeting, or reinforcement of a main point already mentioned. For these instances, a P.S. may be appropriate. As it happens, readers often pay more attention to the P.S. than to the main text. Some people believe, moreover, that a handwritten P.S. on a typewritten letter makes the letter appear more personal, in addition to drawing attention to points of significance.

Not all readers, however, consider the P.S. an appropriate appendage to a formal business letter; some see it as an afterthought that someone with poor organizational skills was unable to fit into the letter. So in deciding whether to use a P.S., always judge the background and expectations of the particular reader.

Letter Rule #8: Write one-page letters, using attachments for details.

Many people in business prefer the one-page letter, which is reason enough to try your best to write one. Letters are only complements to personal contacts with clients, not replacements for them, so there is not much reason to write more than a page. When you have a lot to say, attachments help shorten the letter text. They also help you separate main points in the letter text from less important supporting details. For example, a letter suggesting two alternatives to solving an accounting problem could *highlight* the alternatives in the letter and *describe* the alternatives in two attachments.

But sometimes a letter must run longer than a page. You may be answering a series of questions posed by the reader or presenting a series of benefits. In these cases, try to end pages with a comment or rhetorical question that encourages the reader to turn to the next page. A question like "Just how much will you save with this new inventory technique?" might come right before a page change, for example.

Letter Rule #9: Use the letter format your readers prefer.

Many writers dismiss the selection of letter styles or formats (block, modified block, or simplified) as inconsequential. They tend to use the style most familiar to their secretaries or firm. But this approach misses an opportunity to show clients you are ready to meet their standards. You should instead match your letter style to theirs.

Differences among the main letter styles are largely mechanical and can be mastered quickly. The sample sales letters at the end of this chapter demonstrate these options:

- Block style (Example #1)
- Modified block style (two versions—Example #2 and Example #3)
- Simplified style (Example #4)

Letter Rule #10: Edit carefully.

Most readers will not tolerate grammatical or mechanical errors, especially in a short sales letter. Just as important as grammar and mechanics in this editing process is attention to style. Write a business letter in language that is close to speaking, avoiding stilted phrases like "per your request" and "enclosed please find." Consider your letter an extension of your conversation. (For specific guidelines on correct grammar and natural style, consult Chapter 8.)

Four Examples and Critiques

This section includes models of four well-written sales letters. To show how the letters accomplish their purpose, we discuss each one in terms of the letter's style (block, modified block, or simplified), the letter itself (with marginal remarks), and a summary critique. (All personal and company names are fictional.)

Example #1: Letter Before First Phone Call. This "cold-call" letter (p. 48) is done in full-block style. Note that all the following letter parts begin at the left margin: date line, inside address, salutation, letter paragraphs, closing, name/title or department, and initials. Although full-block letters look a bit unbalanced to some readers, the style is both traditional and easy to type because of the consistent left-margin alignment.

Critique of Letter #1. Sending your first letter to a potential client is a lot like sending a job letter and résumé: the only purpose is to get your foot in the door. Peterson wants to interest Taft just enough to get the phone conversation going next week, thus paving the way for a first meeting.

Paragraph #1: Peterson will probably capture Taft's interest, for he immediately introduces a word of great concern to bankers: *risk.* Also, he uses the question pattern, which encourages readers to read on to find the answer. Finally, he briefly mentions the solution—an environmental survey—that will be discussed in the letter. In just two sentences, he has captured interest and projected the points to come.

Paragraph #2: The two middle paragraphs persuade by elaborating on the problem and suggesting a solution. Taft learns that his savings and loan makes commercial loans in a state with a massive hazardous waste problem. Then he discovers that foreclosure, usually considered the main way to reduce losses, can actually increase them.

Paragraph #3: It's Jones Engineering to the rescue. Peterson uses three bulleted points to indicate how an environmental survey can help eliminate Foust's liability. He also includes the good selling point that these surveys usually take only a couple of weeks, because he knows that Taft will not want the survey process to extend closings on commercial properties.

Paragraph #4: Peterson remains in control of the sales process by mentioning that he will call the next week for an appointment. His language is important: note that he states the purpose from the client's point of view, not his own. He wants to "find out if our site surveys can help Foust Savings and Loan reduce its liability." Peterson remains the helper, not the salesman. Of course, Taft knows that Peterson seeks a major contract that could result in dozens of site surveys and thousands of dollars. But the letter avoids the kind of self-serving tone that might arouse Taft's suspicions.

Example #2: Letter After Phone Call. This model (p. 49) is written in one version of modified block. It differs from full block in that three parts— dateline, closing, and name/title or department—are indented, much as they would be in a friendly letter. All three are indented the same number of spaces, usually starting about halfway across the page.

Jones Engineering, Inc.

Geotechnical Consultants

213 Spring Street
Hardyville, Texas 77766

March 4, 19XX

Mr. Howard Taft, President
Foust Savings and Loan
23 Forge Avenue
Strutney, Texas 77112

Dear Mr. Taft:

Did you know that when you make a loan on industrial
property where hazardous waste is disposed, your risk
may exceed property value? Fortunately, there _is_ a way
to predict your risk: an environmental survey.

For the past 40 years, Gulf Coast plants have generated
over 25% of the nation's hazardous waste. Most of that
material is buried or dumped at sites near its origin.
If your bank unknowingly holds a lien on a location
where such wastes have been deposited, you may also hold
all liability in the event of foreclosure.

Conducting an environmental survey before you make a
loan greatly reduces your risk. One of our surveys,
which can usually be completed in less than two weeks,
will

- Identify potential waste problems
- Describe the scope of the needed clean-up
- Develop a cost estimate for clean-up

Mr. Taft, I'll give you a call next week to explain how
our site surveys can help Foust Savings and Loan reduce
its liability.

Sincerely,

Gannly L. Peterson, P.E.
Hazardous Waste Department

dv

LETTER #1 Full Block Style

Write Right! Inc.

Harold S. Reuben, Ph.D.
123 Upp Street
Baltimore, Maryland 22233
(212) 222-6622

May 15, 19XX

Ms. Koro Y. Letson
Bradley Metal Products
202 Jetson Blvd.
Sunnyland, Maryland 21213

Dear Ms. Letson:

I enjoyed talking with you yesterday about your interest
in a sales writing seminar. My research shows that this
kind of seminar can increase your sales from 5 to 10%
within a year.

You mentioned that you wanted some brief preliminary
information, before we proceed to the proposal stage. So
I have enclosed these three items:

- Tentative program outline, based on the needs you
  described
- A recent article in <u>Sales Journal</u> on the value of a
  consistent company approach to sales proposals
- My résumé, including a list of recent clients

Let me stress that the enclosed program outline is just
one possible approach. We can refine it considerably
after we talk further about the goals of the seminar,
the background of participants, and your scheduling
needs.

As you said, your training staff might want to help with
seminar design. I'll give you a call next week to see if
all of us can meet to discuss your program.

Sincerely,

Harold S. Reuben
President

rf
Enclosures

Date, closing, and name/title sections indented in modified-block style

Refers to previous contact (phone call)

Engages interest with significant claim

Responds to reader's specific request

Uses bullets to emphasize three enclosures

Mentions specific topics that will be covered in next conversation, to produce tailored training session

Stays in control by saying he will call

LETTER #2   Modified Block, Not Indented

Critique of Letter #2. This kind of letter must be sent *immediately* after a first phone call with a potential client. Reuben has the client's attention. If he demonstrates responsiveness to her needs, he'll be on the way to writing a proposal almost guaranteed of acceptance. This letter, then, can provide the foundation for a productive meeting.

Paragraph #1: The writer first mentions his previous contact with the reader, then uses one of the ten lead-off techniques to capture interest: a challenging claim that can be supported. His support for the claim "My research shows . . ." might be postseminar evaluations after another firm's course, for example. This support can be presented to Letson later in the proposal process, if necessary.

Paragraph #2: It's important not to appear pushy in a letter that comes between a first phone call and a first meeting. From what Reuben says in the letter, it appears that Letson needs more time to ponder the course and to discuss it with her training staff. She might want to resolve some internal disagreements about the course before Reuben can be brought into the picture. So enclosing the three relevant documents—tentative program outline, journal article, and résumé—is a good idea; everyone can look them over.

Paragraph #3: Here Reuben mentions some specific types of information he will need to plan a course, namely, data about the course goals, participants' backgrounds, and Letson's scheduling concerns. These three topics may form an outline for a future conversation.

Paragraph #4: Reuben remains in control of the proposal process with the obligatory promise to call "next week." He gives Letson a week because he knows she needs time to consider the project before proceeding. A premature call might alienate her.

Example #3: Letter After a Meeting. Like Example #2, this sales letter is written in modified block style. Dateline, closing, and name/title or department items are indented at least halfway across the page. This version of modifed block, however, also indents the first line of each paragraph five spaces.

Critique of Letter #3. Like Orley, you sometimes have the good fortune to help the client design the request for proposal (RFP). That situation is close to heaven in the world of proposals, in that (1) clients often feel inclined to hire the company that helped them figure out what they wanted, and (2) anyone on this kind of inside track probably suggested RFP items to which its firm would be best able to respond.

Paragraph #1: Orley hasn't finalized this deal and has the sense not to appear overconfident. Instead, he alludes to the progress made at the meeting, a remark that helps cement his relationship with the clients. They are

BEST AWARDS, INC.

707 First Avenue   Bee, Maine 04285

(303) 311-3533

June 4, 19XX

Mr. Jay Seuss, Manager of Human Resources
Caroline Department Stores, Inc.
25 King Street
Charte, Vermont 05827

Dear Jay:

The three of us made real headway last Monday in
defining the kind of service award program you want. I'd
like to summarize our work so far and answer a question
you posed about the logo.

You and Hal obviously feel strongly that improved
service awards can help build morale among Caroline's
3,000 employees throughout the Southeast. In particular,
the awards help build and maintain loyalty among
employees who work far from the corporate headquarters.

Your preferences, as I understand them, can be
placed in five general groupings:

- 5 Years: Cross Pen & Pencil (with logo)
- 10 Years: Ruby Logo Pin & $500
- 15 Years: Emerald Logo Pin & $1000
- 20 Years: Diamond Logo Pin & $1500
- 25, 30, 35, and 40 Years: Special Gifts

The design and price range of the pins and the special
gifts would need to be addressed in any proposals you
solicit from my firm or others.

Jay, as for your concern about reproducing the
logo, our designers always work from the precise specs
you have on file. In fact, we ask you to sign off on the
quality of the reproduced logo before we proceed to
develop a master and, of course, before you make any
payment. That way you're totally protected.

From what you said in our meeting, you will soon
select the gift groupings and request bid proposals from
Best and perhaps other firms. In the meantime, please
call if you need any more help preparing the request for
proposal.

Sincerely,

George W. Orley
V.P., Northeast
Region

vh

LETTER #3 Modifed Block, Indented

probably beginning to view Best as a member of their "team." Then he captures interest by projecting the content of the letter: it will summarize the results of the meeting and answer a question that Seuss posed.

Paragraph #2: Orley writes convincingly here. By summarizing the main conclusions of the meeting, he reinforces Caroline's inclination to adopt a major service awards program. Orley knows the firm needs this program to build morale, particularly at the small stores in outlying locations; he also knows that a comprehensive program will bring his firm the greatest profit.

Paragraph #3: This listing of the five award categories is basically "for the record." It prevents later disagreement about what groupings were discussed. With agreement on these categories, Orley may decide to have his design staff do some preliminary work on drawings and prices.

Paragraph #4: In the meeting, Seuss expressed concern about the quality of the logo reproduction on the awards, because he knows that the company's founder and president (who designed the logo in 1939) will tolerate no departures from original specifications. The letter reassures Seuss that he can approve the reproduction and the model before any money is paid.

Paragraph #5: Because the RFP will be forthcoming and Orley will surely be on the list, there is no need for him to call the client. Indeed, this is a good time for him to back off and hope that all his efforts will pay dividends after the proposal is in. Orley ends by suggesting that Seuss give him a call if he needs any more help developing the RFP. It is usually poor strategy to end with a "call me if you have questions" sentence, but it is appropriate here, since control has been established in other ways.

Example #4: Letter of Reacquaintance. This final example is written in the simplified format, the third major letter style (besides the block and modified block styles demonstrated in previous examples). Simplified letters usually have these features:

- No salutation
- Subject line in full capitals
- Reader's name included in the first line or two
- No closing
- Indenting much like block style

Readers who use this style prefer its less formal appearance and breezy effect, and it is also useful when the reader's name isn't known. But to some, such letters can appear too informal and impersonal. When you are not certain about your reader's stylistic preference, it is best to stay with the traditional block or modified block formats.

ALLIED SAFETY ENGINEERING

388 Kister Avenue
Seebrook, Oregon 97028
(808) 344-5656

August 21, 19XX

Mr. James Swartz, Safety Director
Jessup County School System
1111 Clay Street
Smiley, Oregon 97666

NEW ASBESTOS ABATEMENT SERVICE NOW AVAILABLE

We enjoyed working with you last year, James, to update
your entire fire alarm system. Given the current concern
in the country about another safety issue, asbestos, we
wanted you to know that our staff now does abatement
work.

As you know, many of the state's school systems were
constructed during years when asbestos was used as a
primary insulator. No one knew then, of course, that the
material can cause illness and even premature death for
those who work in buildings where asbestos was used in
construction. Now we know that just a small portion of
asbestos produces a major health hazard.

Fortunately, there's a way to tell if you have a
problem: the asbestos survey. This procedure, done by
our certified asbestos-abatement professionals, results
in a report that tells whether or not your buildings are
affected. And if we find asbestos, we can remove it for
you.

Jessup showed real foresight in modernizing its alarm
system last year, James. Your desire for a thorough job
on that project was matched, as you know, by the
approach we take to our business. Now we'd like to help
give you the peace of mind that will come from knowing
that either (1) there is no asbestos problem in your 35
structures or (2) you have removed the material.

The enclosed brochure outlines our asbestos services.
I'll give you a call in a few days to see if Allied can
help you out.

Ben

Benjamin R. Statler
Project Manager

nb
Enclosure

Critique of Letter #4. Remember, your best opportunity for business often flows from the good work you've already done. Statler is wise to write Swartz while the alarm project is still fresh in the client's mind. Chances are that Swartz will see all that is offered in this letter in light of the professional job Allied did on the alarms. Always try for repeat business when the last association was a good one.

Paragraph #1: The writer wastes no time reminding the reader of the successful work performed last year, but doesn't belabor the point. Instead, he moves quickly to the purpose of the letter—to describe Allied's new asbestos service. Mentioning the word "asbestos" to someone charged with the safety of many people will certainly capture interest. Statler does so without resorting to needless fear mongering.

Paragraph #2: Here Statler relates the problem to the Jessup County School System. First, he notes that many of the schools were built when asbestos was used in construction; then he explains that the material can affect those within the structures long after construction.

Paragraph #3: This paragraph's first sentence makes clear what Allied can do for Jessup: a diagnostic survey and, if necessary, cleanup. It's important that Statler convey the sense that Allied can handle the whole problem.

Paragraph #4: Statler reinforces an already established theme of the professionalism that Allied brings to its jobs. In fact, this theme is the central selling point of the letter. He also uses the phrase "peace of mind" to convey the need for immediate action to resolve the potential problem.

Paragraph #5: The last paragraph uses two good techniques. First, it mentions that an enclosed brochure contains further information. Second, it refers to an upcoming phone call as something that will serve the client. He wants to help Swartz identify and solve the problem, not just get a project for his firm.

SUMMARY

This book defines *sales letters* as any correspondence between you and a client during the proposal process. These letters have three main purposes: to reinforce points already mentioned on the phone or in person, to follow up questions asked by the client, and to maintain your control of the proposal process. Follow these ten guidelines when writing sales letters:

1. Use the diamond-shaped rhetorical pattern
2. Use the 3-Cs pattern to gain and keep reader interest
3. Capture interest with a strong first paragraph
4. Convince readers in the body paragraphs

5. Control the next move with the final paragraph
6. Break up body paragraphs for easy reading
7. Add a postscript for special attention
8. Write one-page letters, using attachments for details
9. Use the letter format your readers prefer
10. Edit carefully

EXERCISES

Follow the procedure listed below to establish a context for Exercises 1–5.

Select a product or service with which you are reasonably familiar, on the basis of your work experience, research, or interests.

Assume that you are responsible for marketing this product or service to Mr. Harry Black of ABC, Inc.

Assume that Black is aware of your firm but has not done business with it.

Answer the audience-analysis questions in Chapter 2 regarding Black. Use real or fictitious information, depending on whether you have an actual person in mind.

1. *Introductory sales letter*

Write Black a "cold-call" letter in which you mention a need, introduce your product or service, and suggest the next step in the marketing cycle.

2. *Sales letter after a phone call*

In a phone call you made after the cold-call letter, Black showed some initial interest in your product or service. In fact, you managed to set up a meeting for two weeks from today (he'll be out of town next week). Now write a follow-up letter in which you summarize the conversation, confirm the meeting, and offer additional information that will keep his interest.

3. *Sales letter after a successful meeting*

You've met with Black, and the meeting was a success; he wants you to give him a proposal within the next month. You plan to submit it in about three weeks. Now write a follow-up letter that thanks him for the opportunity to submit the proposal, mentions the planned submission date, gives him more information about your ability to satisfy his needs, and generally reinforces the good relationship that has been started.

4. *Sales letter after proposal acceptance*

Congratulations! After several meetings and one negotiation session, Black's firm has accepted your proposal, and you will begin work soon. But writing a letter right now would even further convince Black that he made the right decision. Write this letter of reinforcement.

5. *Sales letter seeking repeat business*

It has been six months since you successfully completed the job for Black and his firm, ABC, Inc. You know your best chance for business is with satisfied customers, so you decide to write Black again. Offer him (1) the same product or service, or (2) something new that you think he may need. Make sure the letter ends with a clear next step.

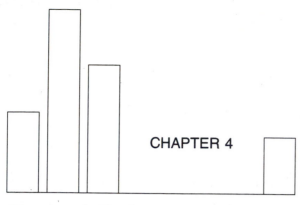

CHAPTER 4

Formal Sales Proposals

OBJECTIVES

- ○ Review and add to your familiarity with relevant terms
- ○ Learn about recent changes in the way companies handle proposal writing
- ○ Familiarize yourself with requests for proposals (RFPs) and the criteria for your decision to submit a proposal
- ○ Learn rules for content and format
- ○ Examine a model of a formal sales proposal (with marginal comments and a summary evaluation)
- ○ Practice the chapter's writing guidelines

Successful sales proposals require that you understand the marketing cycle (Chapter 1), master the writing process (Chapter 2), and write persuasive sales letters before and after the proposal (Chapter 3). If your proposal is due next week, however, you may not have time to read those chapters. So the next two chapters include self-contained sets of guidelines to consult while you write formal and informal sales proposals.

Key Terms

Besides reviewing some proposal types, this section defines formal sales proposals and identifies the information they contain.

Review of Proposal Types. Proposals can be classified in four overlapping ways.

1. They are *solicited* (requested) or *unsolicited* (unrequested).
2. They are directed to someone in your company *(in-house)* or someone at another firm *(external)*.
3. They propose either funding for a research project *(grant proposal)*, support for an internal change in procedures *(planning proposal)*, or purchase of a product, service, or idea *(sales proposal)*.
4. They are in letter or memorandum form *(informal)* or in longer bound form with many sections *(formal)*.

Definition of Formal Sales Proposals. This chapter focuses on proposals that are external, sales-oriented, formal, and either solicited or unsolicited. For simplicity, we will call them *formal sales proposals.* (Chapter 5 covers informal sales proposals.)

Like formal reports, formal sales proposals are bound documents that contain many separate sections. The number and nature of these sections vary from company to company. Write formal, not informal, sales proposals when one or more of these conditions exist:

○ The text of the proposal (not including attachments) is more than five pages long.

○ The scope of the proposed project or the dollar amount of the sale justifies a formal response, thus showing the client the importance with which you view the contract.

○ The client, for whatever reason, prefers the formal proposal format.

If, after applying these criteria, you are still in doubt about the appropriate format, write a formal proposal. It is far better to err on the side of formality. Besides, the distinct sections of a formal proposal make it easier to read and more visually impressive than a letter proposal.

Contents of Formal Sales Proposals. Four terms encompass the types of information in formal sales proposals. No matter what actual headings are used, most formal sales proposals include a *rationale* as well as *technical, management,* and *cost information.*

○ *Rationale:* This part of the proposal describes the need for what is being proposed. It answers one main question for the client: "What does this proposal have to do with me and my company?"

- *Technical information:* The technical section explains exactly what you are proposing in whatever level of detail is required. This section describes your *product* (e.g., tractor line, landscape plan, drill bits, or software package), *service* (e.g., geoscience consulting, computer hardware maintenance, architectural design, writing seminars), or *idea* (e.g., redesign of an air conditioning system, new software package for inventory control, new board game for the over-40 crowd).

- *Management information:* The management section explains exactly how and when the work will be done and by whom. Most proposals require a good deal of emphasis on scheduling, with visual aids showing the projected course of the project. If the proposed work involves persons outside the client firm, the management section or related appendices often contain résumés and a chart showing reporting relationships.

- *Cost information:* The cost section shows the bottom line: what will the client pay for this product, service, or idea? If technical options are presented in the proposal, what are the cost differences? What unknowns or variables could affect cost?

Recent Changes

Formal sales proposals have been around a long time. Companies that do government work—like aerospace or ship-building firms, for example—have always written mammoth proposals to get mammoth contracts. Recently many small and medium-sized companies have also moved into the business of writing formal proposals. There are three reasons for this shift:

- Most commercial (nongovernment) markets are more competitive than ever. Work formerly secured by a handshake or phone call now requires competitive bidding and formal proposals.

- Many more producers of products and services are competing for government work that requires formal written proposals.

- Professionals, particularly engineers, now see proposal writing as part of their jobs, whereas a few years ago it was viewed as an unsuitable activity for technical people. Clients now prefer to deal with technical experts who have good marketing skills, rather than with marketing experts who have only superficial technical knowledge.

On the last point, I saw the change occur over a five-year period in one oil-related firm that hired me to teach writing seminars. During the first year, the company wanted courses with little (if any) emphasis on proposal writing. This prospering firm was mainly concerned with the quality of its project reports. During the next few years, however, increased competition brought about new interest in proposal writing. The demands of the marketplace caused many technical professionals to redefine their role. They now assumed much of the responsibility for *getting* work as well as *doing* it.

This chapter assumes that those who thoroughly understand the product or service will be writing, or at least helping to write, the formal sales proposal. Other people may be involved, and usually are, but major writing responsibility will rest on the shoulders of those who know most about what is being proposed.

RFPs and the Decision to Propose

In this section we will review the difference between unsolicited and solicited sales proposals, examine a sample request for proposal (RFP), suggest ten criteria for deciding to write the proposal, and offer three recommendations for responding to RFPs.

Unsolicited vs. Solicited Context. The writing guidelines later in this chapter apply to both solicited and unsolicited proposals. Unsolicited proposals are launched on the hope that the clients will suddenly realize they need what you are proposing. Solicited proposals, however, are usually preceded by a great deal of client contact in the form of:

- Letters and meetings
- A formal request for proposal from the client

Solicited proposals offer the best chance for success because they allow you to get to know the clients' needs before the proposal hits their desks. When you have the choice, devote most of your time to solicited proposals.

RFP Formats and Sample RFP. Depending on the size of the project and your relationship with the client, the request to write a proposal may come in many forms: a phone call, a comment during a meeting, short letters, or a written request for proposal (RFP). Written RFPs are the norm for formal sales proposals.

The RFP describes exactly what you are to propose, often covering (1) what questions to address in the proposal and (2) what format to use. The following sample RFP gives an idea of the amount of technical detail that may be requested. It is written in the jumbled, randomly organized manner of many RFPs. You must always read RFPs *very* carefully to ferret out the clients' main concerns. Following is an example of a request for proposal. The lines would not be numbered in an actual proposal; they are shown here to help us discuss the points in the proposal later.

CITY OF CARBONDALE
P.O. BOX 1234
CARBONDALE, CALIFORNIA 99444

Request for Proposal
Services: Removing Asbestos from 10 City Buildings

(1)   Carbondale's Department of Public Works

(2)   invites proposals from qualified consultants to

(3)   (1) survey the degree to which asbestos is a

(4)   health problem in 10 city buildings and then (2)

(5)   coordinate the removal or containment of whatever

(6)   asbestos is determined to be a hazard to public

(7)   health. The purpose of the proposal is to select a

(8)   consultant firm most qualified and interested in

(9)   doing the work. Without knowledge of the scope of

(10)   the problem in the buildings, precise cost

(11)   estimates are not expected. However, all

(12)   proposals should include a schedule of their usual

(13)   charges for similar past projects. The City

(14)   will negotiate a final fee with the most qualified

(15)   firm, hoping that a mutually agreed-upon

(16)   arrangement can be achieved. If such

(17)   negotiations are not successful, the City will

(18)   seek to negotiate with the second-choice firm.

(19)   Proposals submitted for this project may be used

(20)   to select professionals to complete other similar   (Continued)

61

(21)   projects and may result in more than one contract

(22)   with the City.

(23)   The entire asbestos program to be completed

(24)   by the firm selected will involve three stages:

(25)   Stage 1: Evaluating the 10 sites

(26)   Stage 2: Writing a recommendation report with

(27)   cost estimates

(28)   Stage 3: Completing the construction phase

(29)   Proposals should address the firm's ability to

(30)   complete all three stages, making sure to indicate

(31)   what subcontractors if any will be needed to

(32)   complete Stage 3. Areas covered should include

(33)   similar projects successfully completed, the

(34)   specific people available in the firm who have

(35)   done such work and their qualifications, and any

(36)   certifications acquired by the firm or

(37)   individuals. Of major importance are the safety

(38)   procedures and techniques the firm plans to use in

(39)   any necessary asbestos removal, with particular

(40)   reference to concern for worker and occupant

(41)   safety. Finally, some reference should be made to

(42)   the number of people the firm could apply to the

(43)   project, and the degree to which similar jobs have

(44)   come in on schedule.

(45)   The two most qualified firms will be invited

(46)   to deliver short presentations on the highlights

(47)   of their proposals. Proposals are due in the

(48)   office of Mr. James Schotsky, City Engineer, by

(49)   3:00 pm on October 20, 19XX. Inquiries about this

(50)   request should be made to Mr. Schotsky at

(51)   678-756-7676.

The Go/No Go Decision.   Writing proposals costs money, which is why we recommend greatly reducing your risk of failure by building relationships *before* the RFP arrives. If you've been communicating with Schotsky for some time about this project, and if you're comfortable with your ability to respond to the RFP, you will probably submit the proposal.

More specifically, your firm should develop its own "go/no go" criteria to decide objectively when to submit and when not to submit a proposal. You can then score the proposed project, giving points for various criteria that are weighted to reflect your firm's individual needs and capabilities. No matter how sophisticated that matrix is, however, it should address these ten topics:

1. Trust: Have preproposal contacts helped to build a trusting relationship with the client?
2. Uniqueness: Do you have special qualifications for the project (personnel, experience, equipment)?
3. Readiness: Are you prepared to devote necessary resources to do the work on time?
4. Profit: Does the profit potential of the project meet your firm's usual expectations?
5. Contract: Is it likely that fee arrangements and other contract provisions will be acceptable?
6. Liability: Are professional risks within an acceptable range?
7. Competition: Do your qualifications for the job match or exceed those of the likely competition?

8. Interest: Is the project an interesting, challenging, and prestigious one for your firm?

9. Goals: Does the project fit within your firm's long-range plan?

10. The future: Might the proposal or project lead to later contracts with the client?

Responding to the RFP. Once you decide to submit the proposal, you need to respond to every need expressed in the RFP. At this point, you (or the proposal team on a project) should brainstorm to extricate all embedded information from the RFP. The resulting list becomes the starting point for (1) distributing proposal tasks to members of the group, (2) assembling a list of clarifying questions to ask the client, and (3) developing an outline for the proposal.

If you were to apply this brainstorming approach to the Carbondale RFP, you might discover these needs and requirements, among others (line numbers are keyed to those in left margin of the RFP).

Major Concerns. *Lines 32–33:* Since one main client concern is experience, the proposal should summarize all your asbestos projects and emphasize work done for other metropolitan areas.

Lines 34–37, 41–43: Another client concern is personnel qualifications such as degrees, certifications, short courses, and specific project experience. Updated and readable résumés are a must.

Lines 37–41: A third major client concern is safety. Schotsky and his colleagues have probably read about the dangers to workers and occupants from even minimal exposure to asbestos. They want assurance that the process will be rigorously monitored. Provide an exhaustive list of procedures and emphasize that your certified industrial hygienist will always be on-site. Also stress your 100 percent safety record in such work. Describe your new technique for sealing off part of a building that is being worked on from the part that can remain occupied.

Other Concerns. *Lines 9–16:* Although the client's main interest is the firm's qualifications, cost is also a concern. Yet it appears from the RFP that a firm would not be excluded because of cost, unless final negotiations failed.

Lines 23–28: The client has broken down the project into three specific stages. Your proposal should probably devote a separate section to each stage, making it easy for readers to find material.

Lines 29–32: The client wants to know what subcontractors, if any, you plan to select to help remove the asbestos. Stress the reliability and experience of the firms you have used on other jobs.

Questions to Pursue before Submission

Can Mr. Schotsky, the contact mentioned in the RFP, provide more information about the budget available?

Is there a preferred format or style for the proposal?

What kinds of buildings are involved, and what are their ages? (Although the RFP seems to intentionally avoid such detail, Schotsky may be willing to give information that would help you tailor your proposal.)

In summary, careful reading of the RFP launches you into the proposal process. If you have done your homework up to this point, organizing and writing the proposal will flow naturally from the preliminary efforts.

Twelve Rules for Writing Formal Sales Proposals

Because they usually concern major projects, formal sales proposals attract a larger, more diverse audience than that of letter proposals. Readers usually skip around in the document, looking for the sections that most interest them. They rarely read the proposal from cover to cover at one sitting. Given this reading pattern, what writing strategies will prove most successful? The twelve writing rules we will discuss flow from these two overriding guidelines:

○ Give *all* readers a sense of comfort—the feeling that they can find exactly what they need right away

○ Repeat significant information throughout the proposal

Rule #1: Use an extended form of the diamond-shaped pattern.

Like sales letters, formal sales proposals should present clients with an "easy-in, easy-out" reading pattern. Specifically, all parts of the proposal proper fall into these three main groupings (not including appendices).

1. Short, easy-to-read sections at the beginning. These sections contain overviews and are read by less-technical readers, usually the decision makers. Included in this grouping are the title page, letter of transmittal, table of contents and list of illustrations, executive summary, and the introduction.

2. Longer, more detailed sections in the middle. These sections contain the details about your proposal and are aimed at both nontechnical and technical readers. Middle sections can be grouped into three basic categories: technical section(s), management sections(s), and cost section(s).

3. One short, easy-to-read section at the end. This section contains points you want the reader to remember, such as a wrap-up of main benefits. It is often read by the decision makers and is labeled "Conclusion."

As Figure 4-1 shows, this three-part pattern takes on a diamond shape. The top and bottom of the diamond represent the beginning and ending sections of the proposal. They present overviews, easing readers in and out of the document. The broad middle part of the figure represents the longer, more detailed discussion sections of the formal sales proposal. Note that the simple three-part diamond pattern accommodates the many parts of a long proposal. Our remaining rules describe techniques for writing all the key sections.

Rule #2: Construct a title page that sells.

Title pages that merely list title, presenter, client, and date are dull. You can make your title pages into attention-getters by

○   Phrasing titles in benefit language. Change "Proposal for a New Pension Plan for Jones Engineering" to "Improving the Pension Plan at Jones Engineering." Change "Proposal for Accounting

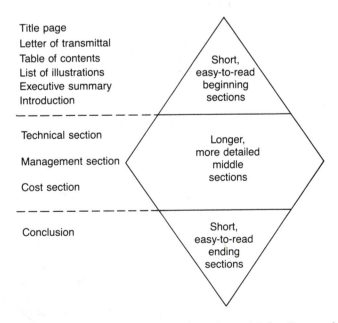

FIGURE 4–1   Diamond Pattern for a Formal Sales Proposal

Data Base Program at Kooroon, Inc." to "A New Accounting Data Base: Cutting Costs at Kooroon." In other words, choose words that convey how your proposal will help the client.

○ Including a relevant graphic. With graphic capabilities becoming more and more affordable, you need to capitalize on the power of visuals. Draw a simple representation on the title page—items such as the product you're selling, the client's building you're reroofing, the offshore rig you're building, or the word processor for which you're proposing software. Such visuals strengthen your message and gain attention.

Rule #3: Make the transmittal letter a sales letter.

The letter must do more than include expected information (such as the person or RFP to which the proposal responds). It must also *sell* your proposal. These are ways to exploit this highly visible part of the proposal:

○ Emphasize one main benefit. What is the most important gain the client will realize by accepting your proposal?

○ Avoid overly formal language. Write the letter as if you are talking to clients face to face as you hand them the proposal.

○ Address a particular person. Always have a contact at the other end whose name appears in the letter's salutation. Never use a generic, sexist greeting like "gentlemen."

○ End with a promise to call. If appropriate, say you will call to answer questions or expand upon points. This call leaves the initiative with you, not with the client. It also gives you the chance to strengthen the client relationship with another personal contact.

Rule #4: Create an accurate, readable table of contents and list of illustrations.

Don't take these elements for granted; they are consulted repeatedly by all readers and can work for or against you. Make them instantly clear in these ways:

○ Use white space generously, even at the expense of brevity. If, for example, double spacing between subsections or major sections will make items easier to read, then add the spacing and expand the number of contents pages as needed.

○ Abide by all rules of parallel form. If level-two subheadings in one section of the table of contents indent five spaces, they should indent five spaces in all sections. Parallel form is a stylistic device that few readers notice—until you neglect to apply it.

○ Triple-check the contents page for accuracy. Headings must appear in exactly the same wording as they do in the text, and page references must be accurate.

○ Separate tables and figures on the list of illustrations. Be sure to include titles and page numbers for all items.

Rule #5: Write the executive summary as if it were the most important section (it often is).

The most important readers often read the summary first and sometimes photocopy it to use by itself. It must give a capsule version of the clients' need and your response to this need. Here are some ways to write a powerful executive summary:

○ Use a clear organization plan. Work either inductively (from major needs forward to major benefits) or deductively (from major benefits backward to a brief problem or needs statement). Both approaches are acceptable, since you can be fairly certain the client will read the whole page, but don't bury a major benefit in the middle of the summary.

○ Stay within one page. Many clients see something sacred about the one-page limit. They want brevity, and it is easier to photocopy the summary if it is on one page. If you have trouble cutting the length, consider single-spacing the summary to get more on the page. Single-spacing also helps to distinguish the summary from later sections.

○ Use a simple style. Write in short sentences and short paragraphs. Use active-voice verbs—for example, "The project includes three stages," not "Three stages are included in the project." (Chapter 8 discusses the active and passive voices.)

○ Use terms everyone will understand. Remember that the decision makers read the summary. Save the technical language for later.

○ Mention all major benefits. Describe what you are offering from the clients' perspectives, not your own. Use "you" more often than "I" and "we."

○ Avoid extensive lists of points. There will be plenty of opportunity for lists later. The force of your argument in the executive summary should be driven by the unity and coherence of your prose. At most, the executive summary might contain one bulleted list of three or four points.

○ Write the summary last. Only then can you get the necessary perspective on the subject.

Rule #6: Use the introduction to build a foundation.

The executive summary provides a capsule version of the proposal for decision makers. The introduction, on the other hand, gives background information for all readers. Follow these guidelines in writing proposal introductions:

- Include a "purpose" subheading. Succinctly state the reason you are writing the proposal; for example, "This proposal examines the benefits of using a video-monitoring system to improve communications on campus."

- Briefly examine the problem to which you are responding. The discussion in solicited proposals can usually be short, since the client already knows there is a need. These brief descriptions should appear early in the introduction, or immediately following the purpose statement. The problem discussion will be longer in unsolicited proposals, because you must establish need. Move long descriptions of the problem into a separate section that follows the introduction (see Rule #7).

- Include a "scope" subheading. Here you briefly describe the range of proposed activities covered in the proposal, along with any research or other tasks that may have already taken place during preproposal work.

- Include a "proposal format" statement. Coming last in the introduction, this brief subsection merely describes or lists the main sections to follow. It serves as a condensed table of contents for readers just before they launch into reading the body of the proposal.

- Write only one to three pages. Though often longer than summaries, introductions must still capture attention. Brevity is a must. As noted, extensive background on the problem belongs in a separate section right after the introduction.

Rule #7: Consider including a problem section to clarify client needs.

As we have mentioned, solicited proposals rarely contain this separate section on the problem. Clients clarify their need in the RFP or elsewhere, so there is no reason for you to do it again. A few comments in the introduction usually suffice. For unsolicited proposals, however, devote an entire section to the need to which the proposal responds. This effort prepares readers for the body of the proposal. Even if you've talked with them beforehand, write the problem statement as if you were starting from square one. You know that your product, service, or idea will satisfy a great need, but your readers need to be convinced!

Rule #8: Design the technical section(s) for busy skeptics.

The technical section(s) refer to the parts of the proposal that provide details about your product, service, or idea—for which you can expect a tough, doubting audience. Your points must respond thoroughly to specific needs expressed in the RFP (if a solicited proposal) or in the problem section of the proposal (if an unsolicited proposal). Four techniques can help sway readers toward your view.

1. *Organize the whole and parts deductively.* Lead off the main section and every subsection with the single most important point in that part. This pattern makes major points easy to find.

2. *Follow the pattern suggested in the RFP or problem section.* For solicited proposals, take your cue from the client. Arrange technical information in the order in which corresponding needs are expressed in the RFP, unless you have good reason to do otherwise. If the proposal is unsolicited, arrange points in the order that you mentioned needs in the problem section. In both cases, repeatedly link what you are proposing to the client's expressed needs.

3. *Use frequent headings as "grabbers."* Make headings specific, use questions when appropriate, and include benefits to the reader. For example, the heading "Can Utah Federal Save on Maintenance?" is preferable to "Maintenance Costs for Utah Federal," and the heading "WriteRight Can Improve Your Reports" is preferable to "Technical Section: WriteRight Software."

4. *Back up claims with facts.* No matter how obvious the claims may be to you, they need support before a skeptical audience.

Rule #9: Balance clarity with brevity in the management section(s).

In the management section(s), clients expect to discover *who* will do the work, *why* your firm is the one to choose, and *when* the project will be completed. These guidelines will help you respond to clients' concerns:

- Display schedule information graphically. Simple milestone or bar charts often suffice (we will discuss graphics in Chapter 7).

- Emphasize what is unique about your firm. When clients start comparing your firm to others, they want to know what you do *best*, not everything you do, so focus on features such as special equipment, special departments, and relevant past projects.

○ Make résumés brief and easy to read. Use the same brief (preferably one-page) and easy-to-read format for all résumés in a particular proposal. Even if you relegate résumés to the appendix, they must still be readable. Also, be flexible enough to change résumé format and content from proposal to proposal, depending on the readers' preferences. Word processing has made format changes practical even for smaller firms.

Rule #10: Make costs clear and link them to value.

Most proposal readers will be suspicious of costs. Realizing this, writers tend to bury costs in long paragraphs and write defensively, which only makes clients more suspicious. Instead, the proposal needs to address the issue of costs with strategy and assertiveness.

○ Put costs in formal or informal tables. Cost numbers are hard to find within paragraphs, increasing the readers' concerns about an already sensitive area. Follow the guidelines in Chapter 7 for creating clear tables.

○ Emphasize value received for costs. Particularly if your costs are higher than average, mention the main benefits the higher costs produce. Don't worry about repeating information from the technical or management sections.

○ Be clear about the cost of add-ons or options. Again, good tables can present complicated costs so they can be understood quickly.

○ Delete the cents columns. First, it's easier to proofread costs without the decimal point. Second, the figure $123,500 looks smaller than $123,500.00. In the competitive proposal business, these small points count.

○ Always total the costs. Don't make readers do the work.

Rule #11: Always end the proposal text with a conclusion.

Readers focus on beginnings and endings, so end your proposal with a punch. With the separate heading "conclusion," this brief section should

○ Summarize the work to be done

○ Stress the proposal's main selling point

○ Assure clients you will work closely with them

The conclusion brings readers back full circle to what you emphasized at the outset—major benefits and the importance of a strong relationship between you and the readers. Just as importantly, it ensures that the proposal does not end with the sensitive cost section.

Rule # 12: Try to replace text with appendices.

Too much text dilutes the significance of the proposal. Include only what your readers absolutely need to make their decision; relegate everything else to well-organized appendices. Obviously, only you can decide what goes where, but here are a few items that can sometimes go in separate appendices:

- Résumés and organization charts
- Company histories
- Extensive graphics
- Exhaustive product descriptions
- Descriptions of similar projects or contracts
- Procedure descriptions
- Exhaustive cost information
- Brochures

Some of this information will be what is often called "boilerplate"—off-the-shelf items that remain the same from proposal to proposal—while other items are tailored to the particular proposal. In both cases, make sure the information is clear, relevant to the proposal, and well organized.

Example and Critique

To write a good sales proposal, you need to *see* one. This section contains a model to use while you write, beginning with a brief description of the context, followed by the proposal text (with marginal notations) and concluding with a summary critique of the proposal text.

Context of Oil Tanker Proposal.   Steve Wilson, a recently promoted maintenance supervisor for Hydrotech, is anxious to obtain a big contract for his firm. His hopes lie with a proposal he has written to Standard Shipping International.

Standard Shipping's RFP indicates that the company wants to give all its hull-cleaning work for galaxy-class oil tankers to one firm, rather than continuing to piece it out to various firms. The shipping company expects to save money by having one company coordinate the efforts; it has also found that a fragmented hull-maintenance program has caused some tankers to miss this important periodic maintenance, which keeps the ships moving efficiently through the water.

Steve Wilson of Hydrotech knows that several firms may bid on Standard Shipping's contract. Although Hydrotech is smaller than some of its competitors, it uses the most current technique for cleaning hulls: sending crews to the tanker location to clean hulls in the water with powerful water-jet devices. Wilson knows that only one or two of Hydrotech's competitors can offer this technology, so he emphasizes its virtues in the proposal. (The proposal is based on a fictitious situation, and the specific Seasled technology that is discussed does not necessarily exist.)

Title mentions
benefit—increased efficiency

INCREASED EFFICIENCY FOR

STANDARD SHIPPING INTERNATIONAL

Prepared

by

Hydrotech Diving and Salvage, Inc.

for

Susan Bard Jackson

Fleet Maintenance Manager

Standard Shipping International

February 24, 19XX

Hydrotech Diving and Salvage, Inc.
Industrial Complex
Belle Chase, Louisiana 70433

February 24, 19XX

Ms. Susan Bard Jackson
Standard Shipping International
Fleet Drive
New York, New York 10019

Dear Ms. Jackson:

Refers briefly to problem

   Your February 1, 19XX, RFP details the need for
improved hull maintenance on your galaxy-class oil
tankers. Traditional approaches to hull cleaning, as you
know, have become costly and inefficient. This proposal
offers Hydrotech's innovative and affordable solution to
Standard Shipping's maintenance needs.

Emphasizes Hydrotech's
main selling point: an
innovative cleaning system

   Recent technology has spurred development of mobile
hull maintenance systems that can be used on anchored
vessels almost anywhere. This equipment, used regularly,
will greatly reduce the accumulation of marine growth.
As a result, your ships will cruise faster and more
efficiently.

Stays in control of proposal
process by saying he will call

   I'll give you a call next week to answer any
questions you may have about how Hydrotech can improve
hull maintenance at Standard Shipping.

Sincerely,

S.B. Wilson

Stephen B. Wilson
Underwater Maintenance Supervisor

sf

TABLE OF CONTENTS

Uses white space and
indention to make contents
page highly readable

LIST OF ILLUSTRATIONS

TABLES

FIGURES

1

EXECUTIVE SUMMARY

Provides overview of problem...

Marine growth on hulls can reduce the speed of ships, increase fuel consumption, and cause more frequent hull repairs. The galaxy-class oil tanker has a particularly large hull surface area below the waterline. If marine growth is allowed to accumulate, excessive drag will occur between the hull and water.

...and solution

The removal of marine growth usually is expensive and time-consuming. Hydrotech, however, offers a hull maintenance system that provides a more convenient, economical way to clean and preserve oil tanker hulls. The Seasled Hull Maintenance System uses a diver-operated, self-propelled, scrubbing and painting device that can be brought directly to your anchored vessels. The primary benefits to your company include:

Focuses on main benefits to client

1. Bottom cleaning and preservation completed in about 100 hours, 30 hours less than most conventional cleaning systems, and

Uses style that appeals to busy management readers—short paragraphs, numbered points, no technical jargon

2. Hull maintenance done at times and locations convenient for you.

Summarizes entire proposal

Because the Seasled System reduces the cost of each cleaning, you can now afford annual hull maintenance and semiannual inspections. This regular attention will contribute significantly to the average cruising speed and fuel efficiency of your ships.

2

INTRODUCTION

Recent technology has made many contributions to the petroleum shipping industry. A new method of hull cleaning and repair has been developed that offers many advantages to oil tanker operators. We believe this new method will contribute significantly to the success and prosperity of Standard Shipping International. Maintaining clean hulls will increase ship cruising speed and fuel efficiency.

Purpose

This proposal will describe the benefits you receive using the new Seasled Hull Maintenance System. Your company will save time and money by using this service regularly for all galaxy-class tankers.

Description of Hull Maintenance Problem

Standard Shipping International operates a fleet of six galaxy-class oil tankers engaged in worldwide transporting of petroleum. Your vessels travel to oceans and ports around the world, where many forms of marine growth collect on ships' hulls. Because the galaxy-class tanker has a large hull surface area below the waterline, even light marine growth will cause excessive drag between the hull and water.

3

Repeats background information for readers who start with introduction

Shows understanding of problem mentioned in RFP but doesn't belabor it, since client already knows problem exists

Furthermore, if marine growth is allowed to accumulate for an extended period, the hull will deteriorate. Marine growth results in slower ship speed, increased fuel consumption, and more frequent major hull repair.

Scope

This proposal reflects our thorough research and over ten years' experience on hull maintenance and cleaning for tankers. Besides relying on our own experience, we have consulted experts at firms such as:

1. Yamamoto Shipbuilding Service Consultants
   Kure, Japan
2. Marine Corrosion Consultants
   Belle Chase, Louisiana
3. Ocean Science Center
   Key West, Florida

The result has been the development of the Seasled System. This proposal explains how using Seasled reduces cleaning time, while maintaining safety-conscious crew procedures. We will also cover features of scheduling as well as the backgrounds of key people who will work on the program. Then you will find a cost estimate, per ship, for both maintenance and inspection procedures.

4

Shows that Hydrotech has done its homework in preparing proposal

Refers to remaining sections so readers don't have to consult contents

Gives brief overview of subsections to follow

<u>Proposal Format</u>

For ease of reference, this proposal is divided into these three major sections:

1. Seasled: How It Will Work for Standard Shipping—which describes the equipment, crew, and procedures

2. Schedule and Qualifications—which provides information on schedules, services, and personnel

3. Reduced Costs Using Seasled—which provides information on the cost of our hull-cleaning service

SEASLED: HOW IT WILL WORK FOR STANDARD SHIPPING

This section describes the equipment and procedure used for Seasled hull maintenance of the galaxy-class tanker. The main services proposed are semiannual inspections and annual cleanings (which include spot painting of bare or badly worn sections).

<u>Time-Saving Equipment</u>

Recent advances in underwater technology have yielded specialized equipment that has revolutionized

5

the ship-maintenance industry. The Seasled Hull
Maintenance System is a self-propelled, diver-operated
device capable of cleaning 400 square feet of hull
surface per hour. (See Figures 1, 2, and 3 for top,
bottom, and side views of this device.)

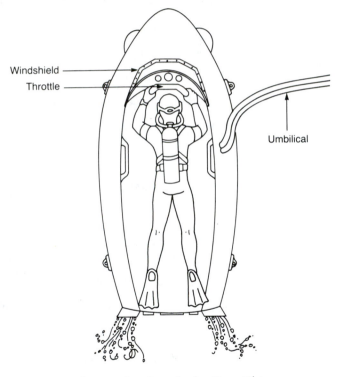

Figure 1   Seasled: Top View

Hydrotech Diving and Salvage, Inc., helped develop
the Seasled System and has used it successfully for the

6

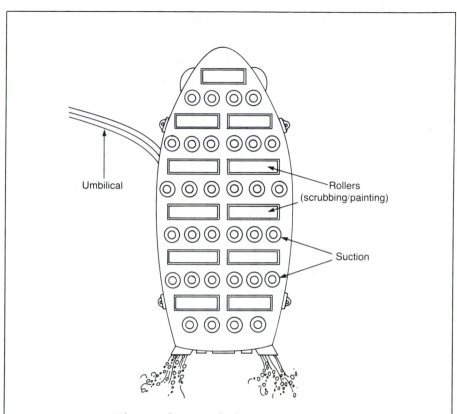

Umbilical

Rollers
(scrubbing/painting)

Suction

Figure 2   Seasled: Bottom View

past two years. The system is quite reliable, as well as
extremely efficient in removing marine growth.

As Figures 1 and 2 show, Seasled is designed to
scrape and then paint the worn portions of the hull. All
power and materials are transmitted to the sled through
an umbilical to the tanker. It's simply a matter of
lowering Seasled and the operator into position and then
letting the device do its work.

7

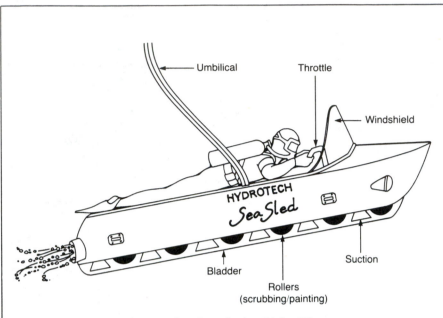

Figure 3   Seasled: Side View

Mobility That Makes Sense

Mobility is the real advantage of Seasled. Any scheduled layover of your tankers can be transformed from lost shipping time to convenient maintenance time.

In the past, tankship operators were often required to take vessels hundreds of miles to deep-water ports where expensive pier space was needed to perform regular hull maintenance. Now our mobile hull-cleaning system can be transported to anchored vessels at locations that are more convenient for you.

You'll also be glad to know that the equipment is easily transferred from small craft to tanker deck,

Explicitly states difference between results from old and new systems

8

using the cargo lifting davits you already have on board. Furthermore, the hull cleaning and paint repair can be conducted while the ship is at anchor in calm water.

Describes procedures with short paragraphs and lists

Diving Crew and Procedure

Our diving crews consist of highly trained professionals who ensure high standards of safety and productivity. A typical diving crew for hull maintenance includes:

1. Two experienced diving supervisors
2. Six certified commercial divers
3. Four vocationally trained tenders
4. Two qualified equipment technicians

These workers are on call 24 hours a day and will supervise the transport of the equipment to the desired location. Once aboard your ship, the system is assembled and operable in less than 12 hours.

Our personnel work 12-hour shifts around the clock with a diving supervisor on duty at all times. The hull-cleaning and paint-repair operation is conducted as follows:

1. Two divers, operating the sleds, start on the port and starboard sides of the bow and work toward the stern.

9

2. Each diver is monitored and assisted from topside by a tender.

3. Two standby divers are on deck and ready to assist the working diver in case of an emergency.

4. An equipment technician monitors and maintains the system.

During the entire operation, a surface-supplied life-support system and standard diving equipment are used by the diving crew.

Diver Rotation

The working divers are relieved every four hours, and the rotation proceeds as follows:

Emphasizes use of safe techniques

1. The off-going divers are off duty for 12 hours following their dive.

2. The on-coming divers are on call eight hours before their dive.

3. The on-coming divers act as standby divers for the four hours immediately preceding their dive.

Completion Time

Table 1 lists individual tasks in the left column and the maximum completion time for each task in the right column. As you can see, the maximum completion time for an average galaxy-class tanker is 101 hours—far less than other methods.

10

TABLE 1

JOB COMPLETION TIME:

CLEANING THE GALAXY HULL WITH SEASLED

Task	Completion Time
System Assembly	12 Hours
Hull Cleaning	75 Hours
Paint Repair	8 Hours
System Disassembly	6 Hours
Total Maximum Completion Time	101 Hours

The completion time was calculated for an empty galaxy-class tanker with a draft of 30 feet and 60,000 square feet of hull surface below the waterline.

SCHEDULE AND QUALIFICATIONS

This section provides a recommended maintenance schedule and a description of services and personnel available to Standard Shipping International.

Schedules That Save Money

As you know, each ship should have annual cleanings and semiannual inspections to ensure that heavy growth

11

does not develop. The thicker the encrustation, the harder it is to remove. Thus a regular maintenance schedule is needed to keep your ships operating at peak performance and to help us complete each job on time.

We realize that your ships run on irregular schedules due to the constantly changing requirements of your customers. Thus here are the two main features of our scheduling that respond to your needs:

Numbered points emphasize how Hydrotech will meet important scheduling requirements

1. Hydrotech will keep a record of each ship's annual cleaning and semiannual inspections and contact you to arrange a periodic rendezvous for hull cleaning.

2. If you need unscheduled work, Hydrotech <u>guarantees</u> that it can mobilize a crew to leave Hydrotech's headquarters within 72 hours of your call to us. This quick response time provides the flexibility you need to keep your fleet seaworthy and profitable.

Introduces related services so client knows Hydrotech is a full-service firm despite its small size

<u>Variety of Services Available to You</u>

Hydrotech offers many other maintenance and emergency services. Those that are frequently required include:

1. Removal of obstructions from propellers and shafts
2. Sea suction and discharge clearing
3. Recovery of lost equipment

12

4. Emergency damage-control repairs

5. Assistance to vessels that have run aground

6. Ship salvage operations

As you know, problems such as these are all too common in the shipping industry. Response time often determines whether schedules will be met, whether equipment can be recovered, or even if lives are saved. At Hydrotech, we respond to emergency calls with speed and dedication. You will receive the highest priority in an emergency.

Assures that Standard Shipping will receive priority service

Professionals That Make the Difference

Since 19XX, Hydrotech has recruited professionals with experience in all phases of diving, underwater construction, and ship repair. Our personnel have the education and experience necessary to ensure safe, efficient, and professional performance for our customers. Some of our key personnel available to Standard Shipping include:

List stresses experience of firm's personnel

- William Baily, Jr., President and Chief Executive Officer, Hydrotech—formerly, Commander, Naval Undersea Systems Center, U.S.N. (Retired)
- Joseph Smith, Senior Vice-President, Hydrotech—formerly, Commander, Naval Ship Repair Facility, U.S.N. (Retired)

13

- John Delong, Diving Personnel Superintendent, Hydrotech—formerly, Master Diver, Naval Diving and Salvage Facility, U.S.N. (Retired)
- Samuel Johnson, Operations Officer, Hydrotech—formerly, Commander, Naval Undersea Construction Center, U.S.N. (Retired)

All crew members are carefully selected by our personnel department, under the supervision of Mr. Delong. The following list gives requirements for specific positions:

Lists criteria to further support claims of company's professionalism

1. Diving Supervisors—selected from our senior divers or former U.S.N. Master Divers
2. Divers—selected from our senior tenders or former U.S.N. First Class Divers
3. Tenders—graduates of certified commercial diving schools; must complete our in-house training program
4. Equipment Technicians—trade-school graduates with at least two years' experience in our equipment repair shops

Our selection and promotion policy is time-consuming. But this policy pays off for you in terms of high productivity and safety records, which are among the best in the diving industry. We will accept nothing less.

14

REDUCED COSTS USING SEASLED

As noted earlier, the Seasled System introduces increased efficiency, and thus reduced costs, to hull-cleaning projects. The charge for hull cleaning and paint repair for your vessels will vary by location, due to transportation costs. For your convenience, we have assigned flat rates for five geographic areas:

- Region 1—Southeastern U.S. (includes Georgia, Florida, Louisiana, and Texas)
- Region 2—the northern quadrant of the Western hemisphere (except that area designated Southeastern U.S.)
- Region 3—the southern quadrant of the Western hemisphere
- Region 4—the northern quadrant of the Eastern hemisphere
- Region 5—the southern quadrant of the Eastern hemisphere

Table 2 lists the charges for hull maintenance and semiannual inspection per ship. These costs are guaranteed through 19XX and include all transportation charges. As mentioned in your RFP, Standard Shipping will provide room and board for our crews on site.

15

TABLE 2

HULL MAINTENANCE AND INSPECTION CHARGES PER SHIP

Service	Regions				
	Region #1	Region #2	Region #3	Region #4	Region #5
Maintenance	$25,000	$30,000	$35,000	$40,000	$40,000
Inspection	$ 5,000	$ 7,000	$ 9,000	$11,000	$11,000

Our portable hull-maintenance system rates apply only to empty galaxy-class tankers with a draft of about 30 feet. Special rates can be quoted for loaded tankers on an individual basis.

CONCLUSION

Hull cleaning on oil tankers used to be expensive and time-consuming. Ships had to be taken hundreds of miles to deep-water ports, where expensive pier mooring was needed to perform underwater hull maintenance.

16

Returns to client's major concerns—regular schedules and cost savings

A new hull-maintenance system, which can be brought to your anchored vessels, is now available. The Seasled Hull Maintenance System uses a diver-operated, self-propelled, scrubbing and painting device. This portable system can clean the bottom of an empty galaxy-class oil tanker and paint damaged areas in about four days.

Our diving crew can rendezvous with your ships at times and locations that fit your schedule, and turn lost time into money-saving maintenance time. To keep your ships operating at maximum efficiency, we recommend annual hull cleaning and semiannual inspections of all surfaces beneath the waterline.

We look forward to tailoring a hull-maintenance schedule to fulfill your individual requirements.

Critique.   We can assume that Standard Shipping's RFP made clear these objectives: saving money and establishing a scheduled maintenance program. The company believes that giving the contract for all galaxy-class tankers to one firm, rather than to the many with which it now deals, will accomplish both goals.

Steve Wilson has written an extremely responsive proposal. First, it clearly addresses the issues of cost savings and scheduled maintenance. Second, it focuses on one central selling point throughout the document: the Seasled System's use of the most current hull-cleaning techniques. Here are the specific ways the proposal satisfies the twelve guidelines for writing formal proposals:

Rule #1: The beginning and ending sections of the proposal are easy to read, with the more technical information contained in the longer middle sections.

Rule #2: The title page emphasizes a benefit by including the words "increased efficiency" in the proposal title.

Rule #3: In the transmittal letter, Wilson uses layman's language to show how Hydrotech can solve Standard Shipping's problems. By briefly describing the Seasled System and its main advantages, he engages the reader's interest rather than wasting the letter on empty clichés and generalizations. Also, he appropriately ends with a promise to call after the client has had a chance to read the proposal.

Rule #4: White space is used effectively in the table of contents. The sections and subsections are evenly spaced over the entire page. Aligned indentions permit the reader to scan chapter subheadings with ease.

Rule #5: Directed to the management readers, the executive summary provides a capsule version of the hull-maintenance problem and Hydrotech's response to it. It picks up on the themes first noted in the transmittal letter and later detailed in the proposal discussion. Equally important, this summary includes short sentences and paragraphs and avoids technical jargon.

Rules #6 and #7: The introduction makes clear the purpose of the proposal, the extent of any preproposal work, the range of information in the proposal, and the format of the rest of the document. It also includes a description of the hull-maintenance problem, since that description is fairly brief. (A longer problem statement would necessitate a separate proposal section after the introduction.) Thus both management and technical readers can rely on this introduction as a foundation for their reading of other sections.

Rule #8: The technical section covers all major features of the Seasled System that relate to Standard Shipping's problem. Benefit-oriented subheadings quickly direct readers to the topics about which they may want information, such as the diving procedures.

Rule #9: The management section first focuses on the main issue of maintenance schedules; it emphasizes Hydrotech's precision record keeping and its quick responsiveness to emergencies, should they arise. Then the writer shows that his firm is broad-based enough to provide related services that may be needed later. Finally, the bulleted list of key personnel helps demonstrate the firm's professionalism.

Rule #10: The use of flat rates per region makes the cost section particularly easy to understand, given the size of the contract. Aiding this effort is the use of a listing (for the regional breakdowns) and the table (for costs per ship).

Rule #11: The conclusion brings the reader back to the major benefits that Hydrotech can provide: mobility, cost savings, and the latest technology.

Rule #12: Although most formal proposals should relegate technical details to appendices, Hydrotech's proposal is already fairly lean. Thus the writer felt the text could bear the weight of this technical information in lists and internal tables and figures.

SUMMARY

Given the competitiveness of current markets, many professionals must write formal sales proposals. These proposals must respond clearly and thoroughly to the client's needs. In particular, a solicited proposal must answer all questions put forth in the written request for proposal.

Formal sales proposals contain four types of information: rationale, technical, management, and cost. Twelve writing rules apply to format and content:

1. Use an extended form of the diamond-shaped pattern.
2. Construct a title page that sells.
3. Make the transmittal letter a sales letter.
4. Create an accurate, readable table of contents and list of illustrations.

5. Write the executive summary as if it were the most important section (it often is).

6. Use the introduction to build a foundation.

7. Consider including a problem section to clarify client needs.

8. Design the technical section(s) for busy skeptics.

9. Balance clarity with brevity in the management section(s).

10. Make costs clear and link them to value.

11. Always end the proposal text with a conclusion.

12. Try to replace text with appendices.

EXERCISES

1. *Formal sales proposal to city or town*

   Write a formal proposal in which you suggest a change in the services offered by a city or town. Preferably, select an audience that could actually be the evaluators. Do some local research and then answer the audience questions in Chapter 2.

   Assume you are writing as a representative of an interested community group. The proposal is unsolicited, so you must provide a convincing statement of need. Fortunately, you have been able to meet once with your main reader, who agreed to read and consider the proposal you plan to submit. Here are three sample topics that satisfy the criteria in this exercise:

   Changing a town's traffic pattern (proposed by a subdivision representative to the city's mayor and traffic engineer)

   Adding a new outdoor sports field (proposed by the representative of several softball leagues to the recreation director and city council)

   Rescheduling city trash pick-ups (proposed in concert by representatives of several civic clubs to the sanitation director)

2. *Formal sales proposal to a college*

   Write a formal sales proposal in which you propose a change in the operating procedures, personnel, physical plant, curricula, or other feature of a college or university. Select an audience that might conceivably read such a proposal. After completing some campus research, answer the audience questions in Chapter 2.

   Assume that the college has formally solicited the proposal from outside organizations. You are writing as a representative of one of these groups.

   Here are three sample topics that satisfy the criteria for this assignment:

Adding a video-monitor system for informing the campus community about college activities (proposed by an electrical contracting firm)

Improving the appearance of all or part of the school's landscaping (proposed by a local landscaping firm that has done similar projects for other colleges)

Adding a degree program (proposed by a professional society representing companies that want to hire students with the new degree)

3. *Formal sales proposal to a company*

   Write a formal sales proposal in which you, as representative of one firm, propose purchase of a product or service by another firm. Select a product or service with which you are reasonably familiar, on the basis of your work experience, research, or interests.

Your proposal has been solicited and preceded by much contact—letters, phone calls, and meetings—between you and the client representative. You are convinced the proposal will get a fair reading, but you also know that several other firms are competing for the job.

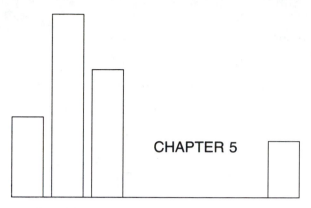

CHAPTER 5

Informal Sales Proposals

OBJECTIVES

- ○ Distinguish the informal (letter) proposal from its formal counterpart
- ○ Learn when to use letter proposals
- ○ Learn rules for content and format
- ○ Examine a letter proposal model, along with marginal comments and a summary evaluation
- ○ Practice informal proposal exercises using the chapter's writing guidelines

Some sales efforts demand that you pull out all the stops and produce a formal proposal, as discussed in Chapter 4. Others require a lighter touch with a less rigid format. This chapter shows you when and how to write informal sales proposals, also called *letter proposals*.

Definition and Use

How does the informal proposal resemble and differ from its formal counterpart? First, both share the objective of proposing that someone purchase a product, service, or idea. An informal sales proposal, however, uses the letter format rather than the multisection, bound format of a formal proposal. The term *letter proposal* is thus often used in industry, and is the term we will use in this book.

Use the letter instead of the formal proposal format in the face of one or more of these conditions:

1. The text of the proposal (excluding attachments) is about five pages or fewer.
2. The size of the proposed project or sale is so small that a formal proposal would appear out of place, perhaps leading the client to suspect that your proposal will be too costly.
3. The client has expressed preference for a less formal format.

Every letter proposal consists of two main parts: the letter proper and the attachments. The letter contains the most important information for decision makers; the attachments contain supporting details. Suppose, for example, that the modest size of your project suggests the need for a letter format, but your outline indicates you will have about nine pages of text. In this case you should strive to *reduce* the length of the letter itself and *increase* the number of attachments, as we will describe in the rules that follow. This change helps readers separate important points from supporting baggage. In other words, give careful consideration to the content of both the letter and the attachments.

Ten Rules for Writing Informal Sales Proposals

As always, start by considering the clients' needs. When they receive a letter proposal, they will expect the *brevity* of a letter combined with the *thoroughness* of a sales proposal, and they will want to find important information quickly.

Rule #1: Use an extended form of the diamond-shaped pattern.

Like sales letters and other proposal types, letter proposals should assume a simple three-part structure. The beginning and end must be short and easy to read; the middle can be a bit longer and more detailed. As shown in Figure 5–1, this "easy-in, easy-out" rhetorical pattern can be visualized as a diamond shape.

Unlike sales letters, letter proposals usually run longer than one page, so they need more body paragraphs in their midsections. Although the body paragraphs should average five to eight lines, varying their length gives visual interest. For example, use short paragraphs—even as short as one sentence—to draw attention to major benefits and other main points, and use longer paragraphs to supply less important supporting information.

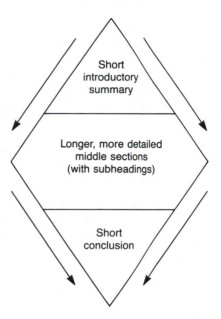

FIGURE 5–1 Diamond Pattern for a Letter Proposal Text

Rule #2: Use the 3-Cs pattern to gain and keep interest.

The 3-Cs pattern works for letter proposals just as it does for sales letters and formal sales proposals. The extended-letter format of the letter proposal requires you to

- *Capture* clients' interest in the first paragraph or two
- *Convince* them in the middle paragraphs or "body" of the proposal
- *Control* the proposal process by developing an ending that leads naturally to the next step

Rules 3, 4, 5, and 6 give specific techniques for applying the 3-Cs strategy.

Rule #3: Capture interest with an introductory summary.

Initially, most readers wonder, "What does this proposal have to do with me?" Give them reason to read on by using some or all of these techniques in the first two paragraphs of every letter proposal:

- Refer briefly to what prompted the proposal. ("Your RFP requests proposals for completing the new west-end parking lot at Sharp Mall.")

- Mention the client's main need. ("Your greatest concern, understandably, is that the lot be completed before the three new stores open.")
- Give a capsule version of what you propose. ("This proposal describes a four-phase plan of construction.")
- Emphasize a major benefit. ("Completion can be scheduled for May 15, well within your deadline.")
- Mention the proposal's contents. ("Described below are the four phases of construction, our qualifications for assuming the project, a construction schedule, and a lump-sum cost estimate.")

It is your option as to whether you label this section "Introductory Summary." A heading may seem a bit formal for a letter, but it does clearly announce the presence of an important overview section. Most readers stop to read a section with the word "summary" in the title.

Rule #4: Use deductive patterns in the body.

Readers want important information up front. They don't want to wade through a lot of verbiage. Writing deductively simply means starting with the most important information. Then, follow up with the facts and opinions that support your initial main point. Use this pattern in (1) each main section of the proposal (for example, "The four construction phases comprise removing the mounds of refuse, grading the surface, applying new pavement surface, and painting the space lines"), and (2) most paragraphs within sections (for example, "Removing refuse from the site during Stage 1 will require about three days and the use of two subcontractors").

The rest of the section or paragraph provides supporting information. A possible exception to this deductive format is the cost section of the proposal, where you may choose to discuss the value of a product or service before mentioning cost. A prefatory description of benefits buffers costs and encourages readers to think first about the value they're getting for the money.

Rule #5: Use headings that attract attention.

Rule #3 notes that a heading is optional for the introductory summary of the proposal. Headings are, however, required for the body. Select headings that engage reader interest so your proposal will stand out from those of your competitors. Use these techniques for wording headings:

- Ask a question ("What Will Option #2 Cost?")
- Stress a benefit ("Using Subcontractors to Cut Costs")
- Mention a client need or concern ("Goal: Completing the Job on Schedule")

Rule #6: Write a conclusion (with heading) that emphasizes a main benefit.

We have stressed throughout this book that readers remember first what they read last. You can best control the readers' response to your letter proposal by highlighting a significant benefit at the end. Be sure to use a heading to signal this conclusion because it separates the final wrap-up from the body paragraphs that precede it and signals the reader that an important piece of information follows.

Rule #7: Place an approval block after the closing.

Make it easy for clients to accept your proposal. Include a few lines such as "approved by" and "date of approval," along with a comment near the end requesting clients to return a signed copy to you. In this way, they won't have to take the trouble to write a formal letter of response.

Rule #8: Shorten the letter text by creating attachments.

Because even a short letter proposal may have many readers with different backgrounds, strive to satisfy all of them with these techniques:

- Place information for technical people in well-labeled attachments
- Place major points for busy decision makers in the letter

This approach also makes it easier to distribute parts of the proposal to different persons, thus saving clients time and money.

Rule #9: Use graphics whenever possible.

Both technical and management readers like to have complex information revealed visually.

- Place simple and/or essential graphics in the body of the letter (for example, a table listing project options and related costs)
- Place complex and/or less important graphics in the attachments

Chapter 7 contains detailed guidelines for graphics. For now, just remember that they should be presented with plenty of white space, usually one page per graphic, unless the graphic is so simple that it can be neatly placed within the text. Make graphics simple and include clear references in the text.

Rule #10: Edit carefully.

Don't let the informality of a letter proposal lull you into thinking it can be less than flawless. In fact, brevity compels you to strive for perfection in mechanics. Chapter 8 provides detailed editing guidelines; here are a few that particularly apply to the letter proposal:

○ Triple-check all cost figures.

○ Triple-check spelling of personal names. (Call the reader's company for a correct spelling of name and title, if you have doubts.)

○ Avoid sexist language. (In particular, do not use "he" as a generic pronoun, and do not use the salutation "gentlemen" in your letter—the letter should be directed to a particular person.)

○ Check the format and wording of all headings.

○ Check that all attachments are included.

Example and Critique of a Letter Proposal

After studying the rules of writing a letter proposal, you need to see how they work in practice. Use the following letter proposal as a model when you prepare your own.

Context of Geotechnical Services Proposal.   James Mason has worked as a geotechnical engineer for Tangley, Inc., for about eight years. Most of Tangley's work is providing consulting services for other larger firms involved in massive construction projects. A wide variety of engineers, technicians, and support people work for Tangley. On its larger jobs, Tangley usually receives RFPs and then assembles proposal teams within the firm. For smaller jobs (under about $50,000), the firm usually receives a verbal request, by phone or at a meeting, along with a written project description. Even though it does much work for repeat clients, Tangley is almost always in the position of competing with three or four firms that do similar work.

This geotechnical and testing services proposal resulted from a meeting Mason had with Arnold Phretz, a construction manager with the large firm of Midwest Constructors. Midwest has the contract to build a mammoth shopping mall in the fast-growing northern suburbs of Yotango, Ohio. In his hour-long meeting with Mason and Susan Lanter (another Tangley engineer), Phretz explained that he wanted a proposal for a detailed geotechnical investigation of the mall site. After evaluating this information during the project, Tangley would be expected to recommend an appropriate foundation design and safe construction methods with regard to the soils and foundation.

Mason knows that this relatively small job will be in the range of $10,000 to $15,000, and thus he plans to respond with a short letter proposal. From his previous experience with Midwest, he assumes the proposal will be read by Phretz, then by a construction expert assigned to the mall project, and finally by an accountant and perhaps a few managers in the firm's main office. (The letter proposal is based on a fictitious situation and contains fictitious names, and the technical content is not necessarily current or accurate.)

TANGLEY INC.,
CONSULTING ENGINEERS
307 Ganner Street
Lanston, Ohio 44060
(214) 424-1237

February 15, 19XX

Mr. Arnold T. Phretz
Midwest Constructors
1212 Fannin Street
Columbus, Ohio 43216

Dear Arnold:

Emphasizes client and his concerns

Susan and I enjoyed meeting with you last week and learning about Midwest's new mall project. Given the varied soils that have been found near the mall's proposed site, we understand your concern that a thorough geotechnical study must precede construction.

Forecasts sections that follow; stresses ability to finish job on time

As you mentioned, your design team needs detailed geotechnical information for the site. This proposal suggests a three-phase program that can easily be completed by the May 18, 19XX, deadline, assuming no unseasonable weather delays. To show how our investigation can meet your objectives, these main sections follow:

1.   Project Description

(continued)

2. Conducting a Thorough Site Study

3. Testing and Analyzing Samples

4. Submitting Thorough Reports

5. Keeping Costs Low

6. Conclusion

Project Description

Leads off with project description to be sure writer and reader have same understanding

From the documents you gave us at our meeting, we understand that you plan to construct a regional shopping mall at a 30-acre site near the intersection of Route 36 and Lambert Road, about fifteen miles north of the Yotango Interstate 285 Loop. The proposed development consists of:

- Five two-story structures for stores
- Interconnecting walkways
- Two stand-alone, one-story warehouses

Although your plan notes that exact building orientations have not yet been determined, approximate locations are indicated on the plan. The plan also notes the approximate column loads.

<u>Conducting a Thorough Site Survey</u>

During this phase of the project, we will drill 15 borings to collect undisturbed samples from the site.

<u>Locations.</u> Deeper borings will be located in areas to be occupied by buildings; the shallower borings will occur in areas to be covered by parking lots or walkways. (See Attachment A for a complete list of borings and their depths.)

Relegates details to attachments rather than cluttering text

<u>Drilling Methods.</u> In line with current practice, we will use the dry auger method from the surface down to about ten feet deep and the wet-rotary method below that. Of course, if water is encountered at any time during the dry auger process, we will stop drilling for a least ten minutes to get information and to estimate the degree of seepage into shallow excavations.

<u>Sampling Process.</u> You indicated in our meeting that you wanted samples to be obtained at (1) two-foot intervals up to a depth of ten feet, and (2) five-foot intervals from ten feet to the final boring depth. Two types of equipment from our Yotango office will be used to collect samples:

Refers to client's own statement about sampling needs

<u>Three-inch, thin-walled tube</u>: for cohesive soils

<u>Two-inch, split-barrel tube</u>: for granular soils

After removing samples from the sampling devices, our technicians will examine materials and visually classify all samples. Then representative portions will be sent to our lab in Yotango.

(continued)

Testing and Analyzing Samples

Uses lead-in "umbrella" for rest of section

This study will require a complete testing and analysis program to develop appropriate foundation recommendations.

Mentions new lab, but only in context of this project

Lab Testing. Our full-service geotechnical lab in Yotango, just completed in December, will be used to analyze all samples taken from the mall site. (See Attachment B for a list of all proposed tests and their purposes.)

Explains how previous experience and new software will benefit client

Data Analysis. Once the lab tests yield their results, data from the mall site will be analyzed in our Yotango office adjacent to the lab—with the help of our patented software program developed for northern Ohio soils.

Supervising this analysis will be Dr. Harold Moore, our in-house consultant on all boring programs. You may recall that Dr. Moore also supervised the analysis on the Hingley Mall project you completed in Oberlin last year.

Uses benefit in heading

Submitting Thorough Reports

As always, we will give you a complete geotechnical report on all phases of the project. Basically, the report will include three main types of information for your design and construction experts.

1. Details about the field work, lab tests, and engineering analysis

Groups three items to highlight contents of project report

2. Recommendations about suitable types of foundations and approximate bearing pressures

3. Suggestions on any cautions that should be taken during construction of the foundations

In addition, we will call in daily oral reports during the two-week duration of the work.

Keeping Costs Low

We understand your concern that the costs on this project be kept as low as possible, without sacrificing the quality of resulting geotechnical recommendations. Several features of Tangley Inc. help in this effort:

- Full-service testing equipment within twenty miles of the mall site, at our new Yotango lab

- Truck-mounted drilling equipment that can be brought quickly to boring locations

- Experience working on four similar shopping center locations within the last three years, all on soils like those at the proposed site

- A new computerized data-analysis program that greatly reduces the number of engineering hours devoted to analyzing the data from lab tests

These economies mean that we can complete this project for the lump-sum price of $9,500. This low estimate assumes that boring locations will be staked by your survey team and that bad weather does not limit access to boring locations by our truck-mounted equipment.

(continued)

Conclusion

Your needs are clear: you must have quality geotechnical recommendations from the mall site by your May 18 deadline, if design and construction are to proceed on schedule. As we have done in the past, Tangley Inc, stands ready to complete the project on time for a fair price.

*   *   *

Arnold, I'll give you a call later this week to see if you want any additional information about how we can meet your needs. Once any questions are resolved, please indicate acceptance of this proposal by signing a copy of this letter in the space below and returning it to me.

Sincerely,

James Mason, Engineer Supervisor
Tangley Inc.

nb
Enclosures

ACCEPTED by Midwest Constructors:

By:_____

Title:_____

Date:_____

ATTACHMENT A: Boring Depths

The 15 undisturbed-sample borings will occur at the following depths:

1. Boring #1–#5 (five retail buildings):   30 feet

2. Boring #6–#7 (two warehouses):   25 feet

3. Boring #8–#12 (five walkways):   15 feet

4. Boring #13–#15 (three parking areas):   10 feet

ATTACHMENT B: Lab Tests

The lab testing program will aim to classify soils and test the soil strengths.

For these purposes, the following tests will be used:

1. Classification Tests

    A. Liquid Limits

    B. Plastic Limits

    C. Water Contents

    D. Sieve Analysis through #200 Sieve

2. Strength Tests

    A. Unconfined Triaxial Compression

    B. Unconsolidated-undrained Triaxial Compression

Critique. After having discussed the project with Arnold Phretz during the preproposal meeting, James Mason felt that Midwest Constructors wanted to award the job to Mason's firm. Yet he had the good sense to submit a well-written, responsive proprosal to secure the deal, just as if he had tough competition. The proposal satisfies the ten rules for writing letter proposals, as you will recall from some of the marginal notes.

Rule #1: The opening and closing sections of the proposal and the paragraphs that compose them are short and easy to read. The middle sections are somewhat longer, but the use of lists and subheadings makes the body of the proposal flow well.

Rule #2: The "capture, convince, control" strategy is clearly evident throughout the proposal.

Rule #3: Mason captures interest by mentioning the client's primary need (a thorough study done by May 18) and by giving a clear road map for the rest of the proposal, including a list of sections.

Rule #4: Most body sections operate deductively by beginning with the most important point, followed by supporting details. The "Testing and Analyzing Samples" section, for example, first notes that the project includes a complete testing and lab analysis program; subsections on both program components follow. The cost section is an exception to the deductive pattern: the writer intentionally precedes the cost estimate with a persuasive listing of benefits the client will receive for the price—truck-mounted drilling equipment, a company with strong related experience, and so forth.

Rule #5: The proposal uses engaging headings that stress benefits to the client (for example, "Keeping Costs Low" and "Submitting Thorough Reports").

Rule #6: The "Conclusion" heading comes back to the major benefit for the client—quality recommendations by the required deadline at a fair price.

Rule #7: For convenience and to encourage a quick response, an approval block follows the letter's closing. Thus the client need not take the time to write a formal acceptance letter.

Rules #8–9: Detailed information on tests and borings is placed in attachments to the proposal text. The informal table in Attachment A makes clear the locations of all 15 borings.

Rule #10: The proposal has been carefully edited.

SUMMARY

Informal sales proposals are shorter than formal sales proposals and have a less rigid format. Also called *letter proposals*, they usually include five or fewer pages of text along with attachments. Letter proposals are appropriate for smaller projects and when you know that your client prefers less formal documents.

Like formal sales proposals, letter proposals must give readers all the necessary details about the proposed project. Concerning specifics of content and format, follow these ten rules:

1. Use an extended form of the diamond-shaped pattern
2. Use the 3-Cs pattern to gain and keep interest
3. Capture interest with an introductory summary
4. Use deductive patterns in the body
5. Use headings that attract attention
6. Write a conclusion (with heading) that emphasizes a main benefit
7. Place an approval block after the closing
8. Shorten the letter text by creating attachments
9. Use graphics whenever possible
10. Edit carefully

EXERCISES

1. *Letter proposal to a college*

Select one small-scale change you might propose to a particular college or university. Choose a topic related to operating procedures, personnel, physical plant, or curriculum; then write a letter proposal that persuasively puts forth your case for the change. Place yourself in the role of an outside consultant writing to particular decision makers at that school.

2. *Letter proposal to a company*

Write a letter proposal in which you, as a representative of one firm, propose purchase of a product or service by another firm. Select a product or service with which you are reasonably familiar on the basis of your work experience, research, or other interests.

Be sure the proposed service or product is modest enough to be described adequately in a letter proposal, as opposed to a formal sales proposal. Consider this proposal to be unsolicited; however, write it to a client for whom you have recently done some major work. Because the previous project went so well, you're convinced that this proposal will be seriously considered if you are able to write clearly about the need and the benefits.

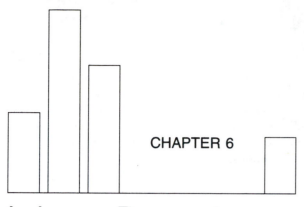

CHAPTER 6

In-house Proposals

OBJECTIVES
- ○ Define in-house proposals, contrasting them to external sales proposals
- ○ Become familiar with sample situations in which you might write in-house proposals
- ○ Learn how in-house proposals can advance your career
- ○ Learn rules for content and format for in-house memorandum proposals
- ○ Examine a memo proposal model (with marginal comments and summary evaluation)
- ○ Practice in-house proposal exercises using the chapter's guidelines

Great ideas strike at strange times. While taking a shower, washing the car, or running around the block, you may suddenly come up with a great way to save your company money. The next day you talk to your boss, who also likes the idea. She may decide right then to make the change, and that's that. (Most improvements occur without a lot of fanfare.) But if your idea goes beyond the routine, your manager will want some time to consider it and may ask you to "put it in writing"—that is, to write an in-house proposal. This chapter covers proposals sent to decision makers *inside* your organization as opposed to readers outside your organization.

The distinction between sales and in-house proposals is somewhat artificial, of course, since all proposals aim to "sell" the reader. Both rely on your ability to emphasize benefits and overcome resistance to change. Yet in-house proposals are distinct enough in content, format, and tone to be dealt with separately.

Definition and Use

An in-house proposal is any document that proposes changes in the way your organization operates. It is usually directed to your boss and other internal decision makers. We will distinguish formal in-house proposals from informal (memo) in-house proposals.

Formal In-house Proposals.   Like sales proposals, in-house proposals can appear in a formal format, as bound documents that contain separate sections (such as a letter or memo of transmittal, title page, table of contents, executive summary, etc.). Such an elaborate format is rarely used for in-house proposals, however. After all, your managers will prefer that you reserve the expensive extras for proposals to a client, not to them; therefore, we will not discuss writing guidelines for the formal in-house proposal. If you should need to use that approach, follow the guidelines in Chapter 4 and consult the full-length model in that chapter.

Informal In-house Proposals.   Most in-house proposals are written in the format of an informal memorandum, usually called a *memo proposal*. Like informal sales proposals, informal in-house proposals are presented with few trappings. They include only a memorandum (usually no more than five pages) and attachments referred to in the body of the proposal. To make the proposal as engaging as possible, try to shift as much material as possible to the attachments. The writing rules in this chapter will help you streamline the text and adjust the format to the needs of diverse readers.

Sample Contexts for Memo Proposals.   Almost any memo in which you suggest a change can be considered a proposal. Topics vary as widely as do companies and the creative impulses of their employees, but here are a few examples:

> Adding a new product line (a software engineer might propose a new word-processing package for correcting five basic grammar errors)

Changing an existing product line (a diaper firm's marketing representative might propose changes in the placement of adhesive tape on infant diapers)

Changing company procedures (an automobile assembly line supervisor might propose changing the method for inspecting spot welds)

Changing company equipment (an insurance company's regional office manager might propose shifting from memory typewriters to word processing stations)

Changing company personnel (a regional sales manager might propose closing one office and opening another because of changing sales patterns)

Internal Proposals and Your Career

Writing good in-house proposals promotes your career in two ways. First, you become more visible, in the best sense of that word. A manager might come to view you as a kind of internal entrepreneur struggling to bring innovative ideas to the surface in your department or organization. As an agent of change, you will be valued within your business, particularly if you also have powerful interpersonal communication skills. Second, the ability to write persuasively sets you apart from the mediocre majority who do their best to avoid writing tasks. Even if your proposal is rejected, you have demonstrated the kind of initiative that few show. The effort will earn you the respect of the many members of upper management who still value clarity and coherence in writing.

All this emphasis on initiative and creativity gives new meaning to a term used quite differently in the 1950s: the "organization man." Today, rather than just going along with the flow, this man or woman strives to set himself or herself apart from the crowd. He or she takes judicious risks and suggests change, and increased productivity often results. Because decision makers are more receptive than ever to this entrepreneurial spirit, internal proposals have never been more important to every professional's career.

Ten Rules for Writing Memo Proposals

All memo proposals share two important features. First, they derive their format from the internal memorandum; that is, both share the conventional "date/to/from/subject" beginning. Second, and more important, both must reflect sensitivity to the political climate of an organization. The ten guidelines that follow show how to maneuver around the obstacles of format, content, and tone.

Rule #1: Use an extended form of the diamond-shaped pattern.

As shown in Figure 6–1, memo proposals adopt the rhetorical shape of a diamond, much like sales letters and sales proposals. Specifically, the memo should include:

- ○ Short, easy-to-understand paragraphs (3 to 5 lines each) at the beginning, immediately after the "date/to/from/subject" block
- ○ Longer paragraphs (5 to 8 lines each) in the middle sections
- ○ Short paragraphs (3 to 5 lines each) at the end to give the reader visual incentive to read the last section

This visual pattern is "thin" at the start and end and "fat" in the middle, like a diamond figure. Readers can move into and out of the document quickly, with the option of reading more detail in the middle of the memo proposal.

Rule #2: Use the 3-Cs pattern to gain and keep interest.

As with sales letters and sales proposals, you can draw readers into your memo proposal if you:

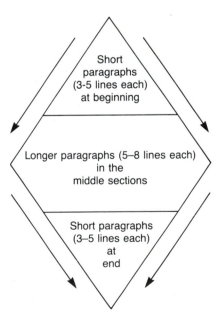

FIGURE 6–1 Diamond Pattern for Memo Proposal Text

- ○ *Capture* their interest in the first few paragraphs
- ○ *Convince* them of your ideas in the body
- ○ *Control* their response and the entire proposal process with the final paragraphs

The next four rules give specific techniques for merging the diamond format and 3-Cs strategy in your memo proposals.

Rule #3: Capture interest with a subject line and introductory summary.

Writers often fail to exploit the subject line and first few paragraphs of the memo proposal. Two techniques will help you engage the reader's attention.

First, briefly mention a benefit in the subject line; for example, "Subject: Reducing Mail Costs by Changing Carriers," instead of "Subject: Proposed Change in Mail Carriers." Make the subject line sell your idea, but keep it as brief as possible—preferably under 10 words. This brevity captures attention and makes filing the memo easier and more accurate.

Second, start the memo with an overview, preferably labeled "Introductory Summary." Similar to, but shorter than, the executive summary of a formal proposal, this section presents a capsule version of the proposal's most important points. It should usually include brief reference to any previous discussions, need for the proposed change, your response to this need, and a list of the main sections to follow.

The heading "Introductory Summary" occurs immediately after the "date/to/from/subject" block. Remember that the section itself should be as brief as possible, no more than two or three short paragraphs; it is only an overview.

Rule #4: Convince readers by including a section on need.

Because most in-house proposals are unsolicited, you must persuade readers that there is a real need for the change you suggest. Follow these guidelines:

- ○ Place the needs section right after the introductory summary. Do not succumb to the temptation to go into detail about the need in the introductory summary itself, or you are likely to have a needs discussion that is too short and an overview that is too long.
- ○ Use a heading that evokes interest. Asking "What's Wrong with the Present Mail System?" creates interest and makes a better heading than "Need for a New Mail System."
- ○ Start the section with an overview answer to the question "Why is a change needed?"
- ○ Use the rest of the section to provide supporting details.

Rule #5: Convince readers by following the needs section with details of proposed changes.

Between the needs section and the conclusion, you must *sell* ideas to readers with strategies much like those in the technical, management, and cost sections of a sales proposal. Be sure to answer questions like these:

Exactly what needs to be done?

What are the main benefits?

How will success be evaluated?

How long will the project take?

What people, facilities, and materials will be required?

How much will it cost?

As in other parts of the proposal, make this section as readable as possible by putting most important points at the beginning of paragraphs and beginning of sections, and using headings and subheadings that engage interest.

Rule #6: Convince readers by thinking and writing politically.

The term *company politics* has negative implications for most people, but in fact you must think politically if you wish to have proposals accepted. Consider the feelings, positions, and company background of each main reader. Here are specific points to consider in selecting the points and framing the wording of the proposal's body:

- View the proposal within the context of the entire organization, as will most of your readers who are managers.
- Be particularly tactful if any of the readers helped to set up the system you are proposing to change.
- Anticipate objections and provide counterarguments.
- Give credit to the readers. If any part of your proposed idea came from one of them, make that point clear in the proposal. Readers are much more likely to support a proposal if they share ownership in it. When your proposal comes to be viewed as "their idea," you're halfway to acceptance.

Rule #7: Write a conclusion (with heading) emphasizing a major benefit.

As we have noted, readers remember first what they read last. The conclusion is your chance to leave an important parting thought in the reader's mind. Use this section to restate the most attractive benefit. You might want to stress:

○ Significant technical features of the idea (if your main reader is most interested in how your idea will work)

○ Main schedule or personnel considerations (if time and people are main issues of importance)

○ Costs (if you know the bottom line is what readers most want to know)

Rule #8: Cut text and add attachments.

Readers expect memo proposals to stay within about five pages. The best techniques for cutting text are to:

○ Place more technical supporting information in well-labeled attachments

○ Use the proposal text only for information that decision makers will need

In-house proposals are often distributed to many readers. Isolating text from attachments allows these diverse readers to find the information they need quickly.

Rule #9: Use graphics whenever possible.

Memo proposals often give you an opportunity to express yourself visually. Chapter 7 covers the use of graphics in detail; for now, keep three basic guidelines in mind:

○ Incorporate visuals into the memo text when they are simple and are needed for immediate reinforcement.

○ Place visuals in attachments when their main purpose is only to supply supporting reference material.

○ Keep all visuals as simple as possible.

Rule #10: Edit and proofread memo proposals as carefully as you do sales proposals.

These are the most relevant editing rules for memo proposals:

○ Keep sentences short and simple.

○ Never use terms the main reader won't understand.

○ Double-check the correctness of all cost figures, graphics, and headings.

○ Ask a friend or colleague to read the memo for clarity, appropriateness of tone, and mechanics.

Example and Critique

A well-written memo proposal will provide a model for your own work. To make the example as useful as possible, we will establish the context of the proposal, examine marginal notes, and evaluate the proposal text.

Context of Sales Training Proposal. Sanford Mertz works as training director for Mudd Engineers, a medium-sized civil engineering firm with fifteen main departments. Mudd recently put all department managers through a rigorous and costly sales training course, conducted on company premises by an outside expert.

To evaluate the quality of this training effort, Mertz also attended the course. Although he liked it, he knows that it was attended by only a handful of staff members who actually need sales training. Reduced training funds preclude giving the course to a wide audience, so Mertz has come up with a sales training plan that would use only in-house talent instead of expensive outside consultants. He arranges to meet with the corporate manager of engineering, Tom Baker. Baker, who must approve all training efforts, responds favorably to Mertz's plan and asks for a memo proposal that he can discuss with his staff. (This memo proposal is based on a fictitious situation and includes fictitious names, and the content may not necessarily be current or accurate.)

INTEROFFICE MEMORANDUM

MUDD ENGINEERS

DATE: January 21, 19XX

TO: Tom Baker, Manager of Engineering

FROM: Sanford Mertz, Training Director *SM*

SUBJECT: Effective In-House Sales Skill Training

Introductory Summary

Using our discussion last week as a starting point, I've devised a preliminary plan for spreading sales training throughout the firm. The goal is to deliver this training quickly and economically, while keeping much of the effectiveness of more expensive alternatives.

This proposal notes the need for continued training and then proposes
one-day courses entitled Sales Techniques, Sales Writing, and Sales Presentations. As Attachment A shows, these three courses can work together to beef
up our sales training program.

Only general features of the courses are outlined below. Details can be developed after you have determined the next step we should take.

Sales Training and Mudd's Future

Last month's three-day sales training course was highly rated by all 15
department managers in attendance. Judging by comments on the written

(continued)

evaluation, it's clear they think we need much more sales training if we're to stay competitive in our traditional markets. As well, they were pleased that the course helped them come up with at least one new marketing opportunity for each department.

Most encouraging of all, the managers said they would require all supervisors reporting to them to attend similar courses—if we make such courses available. That brings us to the problem we discussed the other day, Tom. This year the company can't afford the training expense of running all supervisors through the same training that department managers received.

In addition, some department managers have suggested we go one step further to provide not only a general sales course but also more specific training in two areas: proposal writing and technical presentations. From my preliminary research, these training programs would be as costly as the sales training, if taught by outside consultants.

Our problem, then, is that we have an immediate need for training without the funds to hire outside trainers. The rest of this proposal outlines my solution to this problem: we can economically provide the needed training programs by relying on several in-house experts.

Sales Course: Learning to Sell Technical Services

As you know, I also attended the three-day sales course last month, taught by Hank Wills from Sales Design Ltd. My first suggestion is that we condense that material and develop our own one-day version of the course. Here are some points that make this an attractive option:

- A member of my staff, John Rail, successfully taught a similar course three years ago for his former employer. I feel confident that he could handle this project.
- Sales Design Ltd. has given us permission to reproduce any written materials used in last month's course.
- The course can be tested on a "pilot" group and, if successful, repeated many times.

Of course, this one-day course would not be as thorough as the course taught by Sales Design Ltd. But it would provide adequate time to cover highlights of effective sales and to provide several hours for role-model exercises. The short seminar's main benefit is that we can expose many employees to this training, while removing them from billable projects for only one day.

Proposals Course: Learning to Write Persuasively

As noted above, many department managers wrote in their course critiques that we need related courses in proposal writing. I suggest that the second part of our sales training program be a one-day course in proposals.

Three years ago our in-house editor, Jane Edwards, taught several in-house technical writing courses. The courses were well received and covered

(continued)

reports, instructions, and proposals. With our new emphasis on sales, she has told me that she would be glad to develop a seminar specifically focused on sales proposals.

Jane's work on this seminar also might help her complete two related projects recently suggested by members of the engineering staff:

- A brief set of format and content guidelines for writing sales proposals

- A "standard section" document for sales proposals, which could be called up from the computer files and then tailored for each new sales proposal

Another advantage of this course is that it would provide a forum for both managers and engineers to agree on approaches to proposal writing. Perhaps we could eliminate much of the time now spent on managerial editing of engineers' writing.

Presentations Course: Learning to Listen and Speak

Managers attending the sales course also expressed interest in oral presentations training. A one-day course on this topic would be an excellent way to round out the sales training effort.

Recent client response forms show that our customers have three main complaints about presentations by our engineers and marketing staff:

1. Too often, presenters don't seem to highlight the real benefits of the proposal. Instead they talk too long about our firm's history and its successful projects.

2. The presentations often go five or ten minutes over the requested time limit.

3. Graphics are not used effectively.

Returns to cost theme, noting in-house resources

As you know, two or three members of your engineering staff always give excellent presentations and could help develop this course. Moreover, earlier this year we purchased a new videotaping system that we could use for presentation practice sessions.

Conclusion

Our outside consultant taught an excellent sales course last month, but we need to go further. Let's maintain our momentum by giving three one-day seminars in sales skills, proposal writing, and sales presentations—taught by in-house experts, rather than expensive consultants.

Summarizes three parts of proposal

Good politics: mentions willingness to support Baker, whatever his decision

This memo only tosses out a bare-bones outline for the program. I'm looking forward to meeting with you to get more of your ideas on the subject. Whatever direction you decide to take, Tom, my staff is ready to work with you to meet your training needs. As you mentioned last week, at this point in the firm's history there is no higher training priority than sales skills.

Retains control, saying he will call to arrange meeting

I'll phone you next week to set up another meeting. In the meantime, please call if you have any questions.

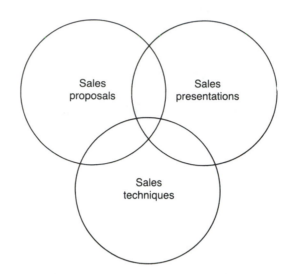

ATTACHMENT A   Interlocking Courses for Sales Training

Critique.   In writing this proposal, Sanford Mertz makes an offer that Tom Baker will find hard to turn down. After all, the three training courses will use in-house talent to teach three badly needed courses. Despite Mudd's need for sales training, however, Mertz knows the proposal will not necessarily be accepted and thus writes it persuasively. The training program will take many employees away from their jobs for a considerable amount of time, which they would otherwise be billing to clients for engineering work. Also, Baker needs assurance that the courses really can be taught successfully with Mudd's own trainers. It would be a false economy to save the expense of an outside consultant only to have in-house trainers do mediocre work. This proposal satisfies the ten writing rules mentioned earlier, as you have gleaned from the marginal notes.

Rule #1: The first and last sections of the proposal are short and easy to read, providing the overviews needed by busy readers. The middle of the proposal, however, is more expansive, giving readers details for evaluating the proposed training program.

Rule #2: Mertz knows that he must adopt a "capture, convince, control" strategy to move Baker toward accepting the proposal.

Rule #3: The subject line first captures attention by stating a goal the reader strongly desires—effective sales skill training. By adding "in-house" to the line, Mertz sets the scene for his points about economy and quality.

The introductory summary also captures attention by linking the proposal with a previous discussion between writer and reader, outlining the firm's need for sales training, and listing the courses described in the proposal's body. Mertz notes the proposal's intended limitation: it provides only general features, not details, about the three courses.

Rule #4: Mertz realizes that his proposal must thoroughly describe the need for the training program. Even though he and Baker have discussed this need, Mertz makes no assumptions about Baker's views, because this proposal is unsolicited.

In the "Sales Training and Mudd's Future" section immediately following the introductory summary, the seed is planted. Mertz shows that comments from the company's managers themselves have made clear the need for this sales training in all three subjects. The section ends with a nice lead-in to the rest of the proposal: Mertz admits that the company simply cannot afford outside consultants to provide needed sales training.

Rule #5: The three main body sections show how the proposed courses can solve the company's sales training problem. Mertz emphasizes benefits throughout, such as condensed, one-day courses; experienced in-house trainers; exposure of many employees to the training; relevance of a proposals course to current projects to establish proposal guidelines and "standard sections"; and in-house availability of audiovisual equipment.

Rule #6: It is clear from this proposal that Mertz is sensitive to in-house politics and knows how to write with diplomacy. First, he mentions that the need for this training has been expressed by the employees themselves, not by trainers. Any other approach would appear self-serving. Second, he suggests that some of Baker's own people, who are excellent speakers, could teach the oral presentations course. Third, he emphasizes the fact that this proposal puts forth only a tentative plan as a starting point for discussion. The reader, Tom Baker, will have the opportunity to design the final program.

Rule #7: The conclusion restates Mertz's most important points: the need to maintain the momentum begun in the sales course last month, the savings made possible by using in-house experts, the training staff's interest in helping with the project, and Mertz's eagerness to meet with Baker soon.

Rules #8 and 9: Mertz presents this proposal as only a "bare-bones outline," as he says in the conclusion. There is no need for detailed attachments. If the proposal had been more exhaustive, however, it might have used attachments to provide course descriptions, instructors' résumés, lists of participants, and schedules for training sessions. The one attachment Mertz does include is a simple illustration, which he uses to reinforce his point about the value of a three-pronged effort to meet Mudd's need for sales training.

Rule #10: Before submitting the proposal, Mertz asked several colleagues in his department for comments on content, style, and mechanics; then he proofread the revised copy three times.

SUMMARY

Use in-house proposals to persuade decision makers to make changes within your own organization. If you write them well, you'll be seen as an employee who wants to make things happen, not as one who only talks about needed changes.

In-house proposals can be either formal or informal, but the more common format is the informal memo proposal. Memo proposals usually include up to five pages of text, excluding attachments. Ten rules apply to content and format.

1. Use an extended form of the diamond-shaped pattern
2. Use the 3-Cs pattern to gain and keep interest
3. Capture interest with a subject line and introductory summary
4. Convince readers by including a section on need
5. Convince readers by following the needs section with details of proposed changes
6. Convince readers by thinking and writing politically
7. Write a conclusion (with heading) that emphasizes a major benefit
8. Cut text and add attachments
9. Use graphics whenever possible
10. Edit and proofread memo proposals as carefully as you do sales proposals

EXERCISES

1. *Memo proposal: Simulated content*

Read exercise #4 at the end of Chapter 1 and use the situational details in that exercise as the basis for a memo proposal.

2. *Memo proposal: Related to actual college problem*

If you are now a college student, select a school-related problem about which you can do some research and write a proposal. Your topic can relate to operating procedures, personnel, the physical plant, curriculum, or extracurricular programs. As the writer, use your actual role as a student. Consider as your audience members of the college community who would make a decision on your proposal. Although you may not actually be submitting the proposal to anyone other than your instructor, write it as if the decision makers addressed were going to read it. Discover as much as possible about these readers. If your audience includes a director of residence halls or an academic dean, for example, you may want to conduct interviews to get some background information (Chapter 2 describes audience information.)

3. *Memo proposal: Related to actual company problem*

For this exercise, use your present or past work experience to write a memo proposal suggesting a change that would improve any aspect of the organization— such as operating procedures, personnel, physical plant, products, or services.

As the writer, adopt the position you actually have or had in the organization, or place yourself in another role if it would make the proposal more realistic. Consider as your audience those managers and experts who would actually make a decision on such a proposal.

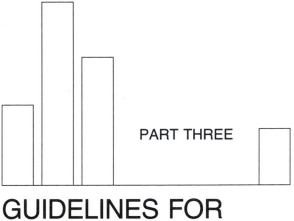

PART THREE

GUIDELINES FOR GRAPHICS AND EDITING

Proposals ask for a commitment of money, time and good faith. So it is not surprising that readers tend to respond emotionally as well as intellectually to what you present. In Part Three we will cover two parts of the proposal process—graphics and editing—that can swing this emotional response in your favor.

Graphics have changed radically in the last few decades. Whereas they were once an optional part of reports and proposals, often stashed in hard-to-find spots, today's decision makers *expect* proposals and reports to contain accessible graphics that complement the text. This new expectation has been fueled by the increased use of computer graphics, making it easier to create first-class visuals, and the growing emphasis throughout our culture on the visual display of information.

Readers expect graphics, so you must deliver. Chapter 7 gives general guidelines for planning graphics throughout the writing process, rather than compiling them as an afterthought, and offers practical rules for pie, bar, line, schedule, flow, and organization charts, as well as tables.

Like graphics, editing has also changed. Readers expect a more conversational style, even in formal documents. Stilted writing scores no points with busy decision makers. What has not changed, however, is the assumption that proposals will have been carefully prepared and free from grammar and proofreading errors. Readers seldom say about a well-edited proposal, "Gosh, what a great editing job!" But they are likely to stop reading a poorly edited one.

Chapter 8 provides rules for preventing and correcting editing errors in style, grammar, and proofreading. We focus only on fundamentals—simple rules to use as you write and edit. Be sure to allow enough time for this crucial final stage of writing.

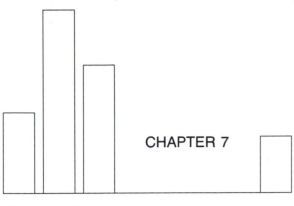

CHAPTER 7

Graphics

OBJECTIVES
- ○ Become familiar with terms associated with graphics
- ○ Learn how to determine your readers' preferences
- ○ Understand the major reasons to use graphics in proposals
- ○ Learn general rules for using all graphics
- ○ Learn specific rules for using pie charts, bar charts, line charts, schedule charts, flow charts, organization charts, and tables

"Write to the art," say proposal writers who rely mainly on graphics to tell their story, relegating text to a secondary role. "Use graphics only to reinforce the text," say traditionalists who maintain the primacy of the words themselves. Between these two viewpoints, you must find the approach to graphics that best accomplishes your goals. This chapter covers the seven common proposal graphics: pie charts, bar charts, line charts, organization charts, flow charts, schedule charts, and tables. ("Storyboarding," which incorporates the design of visuals into the prewriting process, is discussed in Chapter 2.)

Graphics Terminology

Three points of terminology will increase your understanding of graphics:

1. The terms *visual aids* and *illustrations* are often used synonymously for *graphics* to mean any nontextual part of a proposal. We will use these three terms interchangeably.

2. Graphics are composed of two subcategories called *tables* and *figures*. Tables organize numbers or words into grids with columns and rows. Figures take in all other types of visuals besides tables, such as pie charts, photographs, and line charts.

3. The words *chart* and *graph* mean essentially the same thing (for example, "bar chart" or "bar graph"). We will use the term *chart*.

Reader Preferences

When do you use graphics? As always, the key to answering this question is your readers' needs. No doubt your readers have opinions about the relative importance of visual aids. Your goal, of course, is to discover these preferences before you write the proposal. These techniques will help you find out the number and types of illustrations readers may want.

○ Ask in preproposal meetings exactly what kind of graphics they most favor, or, better, show them samples so they become involved in selecting preferences.

○ Investigate the reports and proposals that have been written successfully for the same readers before.

○ Review the readers' use of visuals in their own reports, brochures, and other documents. What they produce themselves often gives insight into what they wish to receive. For example, if they place illustrations on the cover pages of their reports, they may favor your placing them on the cover page of a proposal to them.

Ideally, your inquiry will yield specific guidelines for producing visual material. A manager may suggest, for example, that an in-house proposal for a new salary matrix contain graphs contrasting present median salaries with proposed median salaries. Or, in a preproposal meeting, a customer may indicate a preference for pie charts and bar graphs to show cost breakdowns for your construction consulting service.

In the real world of proposal writing, however, you often don't have time to uncover enough solid information about readers' preferences for graphics and will need to fall back on some general guidelines.

Reasons to Use Proposal Graphics

One main goal underlies all proposal graphics: they should make the document more persuasive by drawing attention to key points, such as needs and benefits. They can simplify concepts, reinforce main points, and grab the reader's attention.

Reason #1: Graphics simplify ideas.

Proposal text tends to accumulate masses of detail, and usually for good reason: readers need the nitty-gritty details of the product or service to make a purchase decision. Fortunately, graphics allow you to augment a complicated textual description with a simple graphic aid. Figure 7–1 shows how a proposal graphic can complement the text, providing an overview of the more detailed idea explained in prose. This detailed description might precede the figure:

> Supertech's innovative Excalibur Abrasive Waterjet can significantly increase your plant's efficiency by replacing conventional cutting tools. The Excalibur makes all cuts with focused, highly pressurized tap water containing abrasive particles. Once combined, the tap water/abrasive mixture accelerates through a high-grade sapphire nozzle and proceeds to hit the work piece at more than twice the speed of sound. Because of this speed, and also because the thin super-jet stream is only .018 inch in diameter, the cut produces an exceptional surface finish. It requires no secondary finishing operation.

The cutaway view gives readers instant understanding of the process described in over 80 words of narrative. It is especially useful for the decision maker who needs to review the proposal quickly, such as before a meeting.

Reason #2: Graphics reinforce ideas.

Many proposal writers assume that the needs and benefits described in the proposal are obvious, perhaps because they have strived to use numbered lists, headings, and other eye-catching textual devices to attract attention. That effort puts them ahead of many proposal writers, but it doesn't win contracts.

Successful proposals also need visuals to reinforce main points throughout the text. Keep in mind that most readers have these preferences for how important information is related to them:

First choice, figures such as pictures, graphs, and charts

Second choice, tables of numbers or words

Third choice, headings, particularly those that ask or answer key questions about proposals

Fourth choice, short lists of numbered or bulleted points

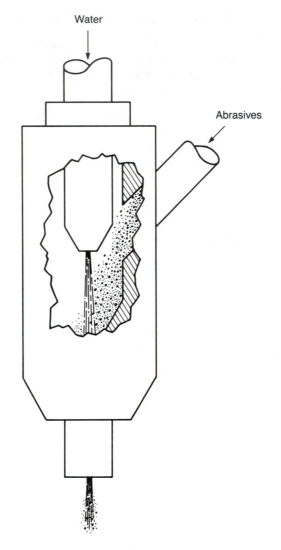

FIGURE 7–1 Cutaway View of Excalibur Abrasive Waterjet—Nozzle Assembly

Fifth choice, short paragraphs

Sixth choice, long paragraphs

Thus, when you are trying to drive home a major need or benefit, you cannot neglect the two proposal components most attractive to your readers: figures and tables.

As an example, assume that you want to persuade a major coastal city to expand its main harbor to accommodate more recreational boats. Your research has helped you determine that in 1988 there were 20,000 wet slips available, with a demand for an additional 5,000. This immediate need for more slips helps support the need section of your proposal. An even more compelling reason to expand, however, is the need you have projected to the turn of the century. The projected need in 2000 will be 40,000 slips minimum and 50,000 maximum. Under present construction plans, the supply will be 25,000 slips minimum and 35,000 maximum.

As you can see by a quick look at the previous paragraph, numbers in paragraph form do not speak very convincingly. To complement the text, you can capture attention by using a line graph to reinforce your point about the increasing gap between supply and demand of wet slips. Note how Figure 7–2 draws attention to the problem and makes the city planning officials more likely to notice the need. Understanding the need, of course, primes them to look carefully at the proposed solution. A simple illustration has helped support more detailed textual descriptions.

Reason #3: Graphics stimulate interest.

Like it or not, we live in a world where pictures take precedence over words. Proposal readers are intrigued by whatever catchy illustrations you put before them. Most importantly, these readers will then move to the text because of the tantalizing illustration you have used as a "grabber."

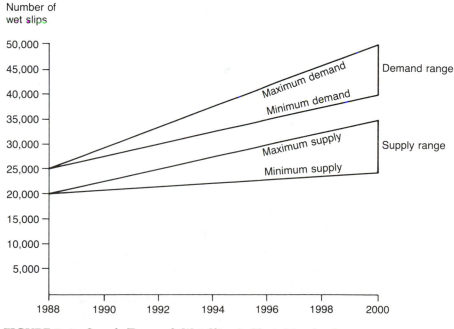

FIGURE 7–2 Supply/Demand: Wet Slips in Hart, Maryland

Graphics that stimulate interest are usually of the simplest kind, such as a bar chart with obvious implications or a line chart that indicates clear trends. These "grabber" visuals may appear anywhere in the proposal, but are particularly effective at these points:

○ Cover of a formal proposal

○ Title page of a formal proposal

○ Beginning of a major section or subsection

Used at these points, the visual aid can entice the reader into finding the supporting information in the text.

Assume, for example, that your firm represents a group of medium-sized companies that want to relocate to a beautiful coastal town in California. That town, you've discovered through research, has an undeveloped coastal area that would be ideal for five or six office buildings. You believe the buildings could be constructed while still preserving the woodsy atmosphere of the parcel. In fact, your environmental consultant assures you that proper design and adequate care during construction will even keep all or nearly all of the bird population.

It is clear that the proposal to the city planning board will be contested by local birding groups that want the parcel to remain undeveloped. You can help to defuse this situation by using graphics that show your group's genuine concern for the ecology of the parcel and that interest the reader in your main points. To start, the title or cover page could include a photograph of one of the species most at home in the parcel, and the body of the proposal might include renderings of the proposal site that pinpoint the sanctuary areas to be preserved.

These types of visuals will confront critics head-on, inviting them into the proposal where you then provide supporting points, such as descriptions of planned structures, procedures for preserving the environment during construction, and supporting opinions from wildlife experts. Graphics can trigger interest in the text; indeed, a picture can make someone *read* a thousand words.

General Rules for Graphics

Some basic rules apply to all graphics. Consciously or subconsciously, most readers expect these rules to be followed in proposals that contain visual aids of any kind.

Graphics Rule #1: Refer to all graphics in the text.

All graphics, no matter how self-explanatory, must be accompanied by references and explanations within the proposal text. This rule follows from our earlier point that illustrations should serve to simplify, reinforce, or make more engaging the prose explanation. In other words, graphics do not exist independently of the text.

There are three main criteria to keep in mind when writing text references to graphics:

1. Always include the graphic number (Arabic, not Roman) when the proposal includes more than one table or figure.
2. Include the title, and sometimes the page number, when needed for clarity or emphasis.
3. Incorporate the reference smoothly into the text discussion that relates to it.

The following examples show the two most common ways to phrase and position a graphics reference.

Example 1: In the past three years, 100 mid-sized electronics firms have shifted to the Accu-count System for recording warehouse inventories. The change to this system has cut losses dramatically, as shown in Figure 3 ("Accu-count Decreases Warehouse Losses").

Example 2: As shown in Figure 3, the 100 firms that have shifted to the Accu-count System in the last three years have cut their warehouse losses dramatically.

Critique: Both examples refer to the graphic number in an obvious way, and both incorporate the reference smoothly into the discussion, but the examples differ in two major ways. First, the writer of Example 1 includes the graphic title for emphasis, whereas the writer of Example 2 did not consider this emphasis necessary. Second, Example 2 mentions the graphic number at the beginning of the passage, whereas Example 1 mentions it at the end. An early reference to the graphic number gives it high visibility, but this placement can send some readers searching for the graphic before they read about its significance. Late reference to the graphic number allows readers to grasp the importance of the illustration before they turn to it. Choose the option that best suits your purpose.

Graphics Rule #2: Place graphics right after the first text reference to them.

In all but the longest proposals, a graphic should appear on the page after that which includes the first textual reference. There are four main exceptions to this general rule:

○ A very simple visual may be placed on the same page as the first reference, particularly if it would seem to "get lost" on its own page.

- ○ A visual that needs to be followed along with the text, such as a complex table, can sometimes be placed on the opposite page—that is, on the reverse side of the previous page of text.
- ○ Visuals referred to thoughout a section or entire proposal can be placed at a central point for ease of reference, such as at the end of a section or in an appendix at the end of the proposal.
- ○ Less important visuals can be placed in appendices at the end of the proposal, where they will not interrupt the flow of text.

Graphics Rule #3: Strive to arrange graphics to be read without turning the proposal sideways.

Visual aids become a more integral part of the proposal when they can be read without repositioning the document. If a visual must be stretched across the page lengthwise, however, bind it so that the proposal must be turned clockwise to see the visual.

Graphics Rule #4: Avoid clutter.

Readers rely on graphics for three main functions: to simplify, to reinforce, and to engage interest. That means they expect a much lesser degree of detail than in the proposal text. Specifically, omit numbers, labels, and other details that are not immediately relevant to your purpose.

Graphics Rule #5: Provide adequate titles, notes, keys, and source data.

Every visual aid, whether a formal table or a figure, must have a title. Place the number and title above tables, and either above or below figures. Center titles or put them flush with the left margin. Notes, keys, and source data are sometimes needed to provide further explanations or to acknowledge borrowed information. Notes contain general pieces of information that put the visual aid in a context and are placed conspicuously beneath the title. Keys give the meaning of abbreviations or terms in the visual aid.

Source data appear at the bottom of the visual aid and cite the person, organization, or publication from which the graphic may have been borrowed. This item deserves special emphasis. You have an ethical and, in some cases, legal obligation to cite the sources from which you borrow information for an illustration. This guideline holds true whether you take a visual *in toto* from a source or adapt it to suit your needs. Your obligation often goes beyond simply citing the source. If you borrow proposal visuals—particularly for an external sales proposal—from a copyrighted publication, request written permission to use the information. Because you stand to make a profit as a result of the proposal text, written permission is a must.

Two final notes on source data. First, it is better to err on the side of excessive notation of sources. Second, consult local librarians if you have any doubts about the appropriateness of your citations. Librarians have or can locate the information to keep you within the limits of ethical use of borrowed material.

Specific Rules for Seven Common Graphics

In the rest of this chapter we will cover the rules for using seven graphics—pie charts, bar charts, line charts, schedule charts, flow charts, organization charts, and tables—that will help you visually present the kinds of information often contained in both in-house and sales proposals.

Five Rules for Pie Charts. When readers receive a proposal, they often first skim through it quickly, stopping only to look briefly at headings or figures that attract their attention. Pie charts can arrest their attention because they offer a comforting simplicity to even the busiest, most frazzled readers. In fact, pie charts are so deceptively easy to use that you must be aware of what they can and cannot do. They show relationships between the parts and the whole quite well, but they provide only approximate, not exact, information. Moreover, they can confuse readers when they include too many divisions. To exploit pie charts in your proposal, follow these guidelines.

Pie Chart Rule #1: Focus on one or two pieces of the pie, with no more than six pieces in all.

The pie chart's selling point is its simplicity, so if you clutter it up, the reader will have trouble grasping relationships. Figure 7-3, with two main pieces among only four different ones, conveys the spareness so important in a pie chart. The eye easily discerns that for this proposed project, Simco will draw most of its workforce from its own offices, conveniently located within a few hours drive of the Hudson, Ohio, project site.

Pie Chart Rule #2: Start your first wedge at 12 o'clock and move clockwise, usually from largest to smallest.

Make your pies more predictable by matching the expectations of readers' eyes. The eye follows a pie chart much as it reads a clock—clockwise from the top position. Figure 7-3, starting at the straight-up position, gives most visibility to the Akron office, from where the largest number of employees (34%) will come to work on the project. Next in clockwise order comes the office providing 25% of the workforce, followed by the wedge representing the Youngstown contingent (18%).

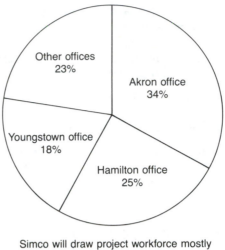

Simco will draw project workforce mostly
from nearby offices.

FIGURE 7–3 Workforce Breakdown for Hudson, Ohio Project

Rule #2 notes that you *usually* move clockwise from largest to smallest wedge. Break the rule, however, if a change in order suits your purposes in the chart. Figure 7–3 moves in order of size until the last piece, "other offices," which is larger than the previous wedge. Here the writer wants to draw the most attention to the workforce contribution, in descending order, of the three main offices. The umbrella grouping of the other six offices is best left in the last wedge, even though it totals a bit more than one of the three main wedges.

Pie Chart Rule #3: Use pie charts especially for percentages
and cents (i.e., parts of a dollar).

Pie charts best catch the eye when they represent items obviously divisible by 100, with the pie equivalent to the total 100 pieces. Percentage and cents/dollar comparisons fit this criterion nicely. Most readers cannot look at a pie shape without thinking of percentage breakdowns. The fact that the circle shape simulates that of a coin also makes the chart ideal for expressing money figures. (Figure 7–4 shows a firm's budget for opening a new office, as a function of the parts of each dollar spent.) As we have noted, pie charts best reflect the relationships of parts to whole, especially when the parts are approximate and limited in number.

Pie Chart Rule #4: Consider using shading, cutouts, and
three-dimensional effects, but don't overcomplicate the pie
chart.

To emphasize one wedge or group of wedges in comparison to others, call out the group in one or more of three ways (as shown in Figure 7–5):

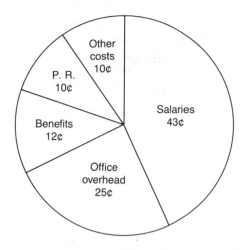

FIGURE 7–4   Cost of Opening Atlanta Office: Breakdown of Each Dollar Spent

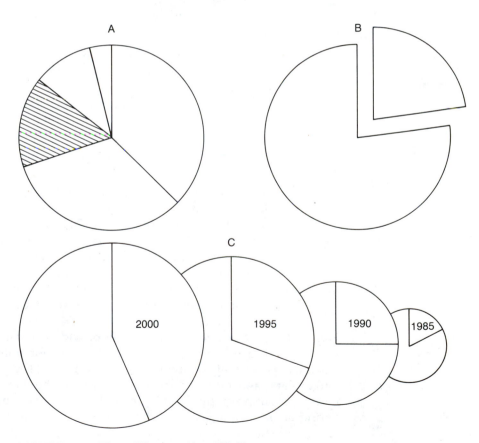

FIGURE 7–5   Three Ways to Alter Pie Charts

○ Shading—darkening a wedge gives it prominence, particularly if it is not the largest one.

○ Cutouts—separating a wedge from the pie chart, as if a piece of pie were being removed, also draws attention to one or two wedges.

○ 3-D—adding a third dimension to your pie chart gives more life to the drawing.

Remember, however, that pie charts should be simple in form and content. The basic circle can accommodate only limited baggage. If you make them too fancy, just as if you add too many wedges, they will lose appeal to readers who are searching for a visual they can comprehend in seconds. Keep it simple.

Pie Chart Rule #5: Draw and label your pie chart carefully.

The pie chart's visual appeal and accuracy are reflected mainly by its size, clarity of labeling, and accuracy of wedge size and arrangement. Follow these guidelines:

○ Make sure the chart occupies enough of the page. On a standard 8 1/2 " × 11" sheet with only one pie chart, your circle should be from three to five inches in diameter—large enough not to be dwarfed by labels and still small enough to leave adequate white space on the page.

○ Label the wedges either inside or outside the pie, depending on the length of the labels and the number of wedges. Choose the option that makes the chart easiest to understand.

○ Draw accurate wedges with a protractor, with one percent of the circle equal to 3.6 degrees (3.6 × 100% = 360 degrees in a circle). Or, consider the pie a clock with 12 segments. Each hour segment equals 8.33% of the pie (12 × 8.33% = 100%). Using the three-, six-, and nine-o'clock points as base lines, divide the pie into the percentages reflected by the two to six wedges. Whatever method you use, remember that a pie chart by definition need provide only rough comparisons, not accuracy to the decimal point.

Five Rules for Bar Charts. Bar charts provide comparisons by means of two or more bars running either vertically or horizontally on the page. Placing bars vertically on the *x*-axis on an 8 1/2" × 11" page allows space for longer bars, and placing bars horizontally on the *y*-axis allows room for more bars on the graph. In either case, bar charts are quite useful for comparing amounts and, like pie charts, are a visual aid most readers easily recognize.

A bar chart variation, the Gantt schedule chart, is often used in proposals to display dates for completing project activities. We will discuss it and other schedule graphics later.

Five guidelines will help you choose the appropriate context for bar charts and produce them correctly.

Bar Chart Rule #1: Use no more than eight or ten bars.

One major goal in all graphics is simplicity. Like pie charts, bar charts will suffer under the burden of too much detail. Focus the reader on the differences among just a few variable amounts, rather than broadening that focus with multiple bars.

Bar Chart Rule #2: Reflect all comparisons accurately.

Bar charts can be abused if the bars are made to reflect greater differences than actually exist. This effect is created by means of the "suppressed zero," whereby the amounts gauged on the x- or y- axis begin at a quantity greater than zero. As a result, differences are exaggerated. As shown in Figure 7–6, a simple technique allows you to eliminate this inaccuracy and still fit the chart on the page. With two parallel lines, make an obvious break in the chart scale that measures the bar quantities. Similarly, break the bars that express the higher quantities. The reader can then easily see that the scale has been broken to reflect a broad range of amounts.

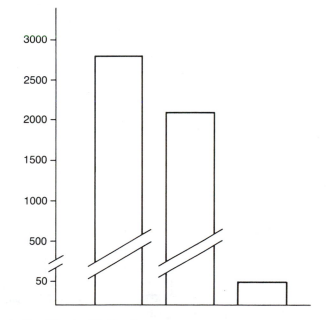

FIGURE 7–6   Bar Chart with Breaks

Bar Chart Rule #3: Keep bar widths the same,
and space bars appropriately for your purpose.

Bars that are exactly the same width, of course, keep readers attentive to the main visual point of the bar chart: the change in bar lengths. The space between bars on a chart is also usually constant, the main criterion being the amount of white space needed to make the bars most visible. Here are some options, with examples shown in Figure 7–7:

○ No space between bars—use this option to show close comparison or trends.

○ Equal space, always less than the bar width—use this option when bar lengths are sufficiently different. Although white space helps draw attention to the bars, gaps wider than the bars take visual emphasis away from the bars themselves.

○ Variable space, depending on the chart's purpose—occasionally you may want varying space to reflect varying gaps between what

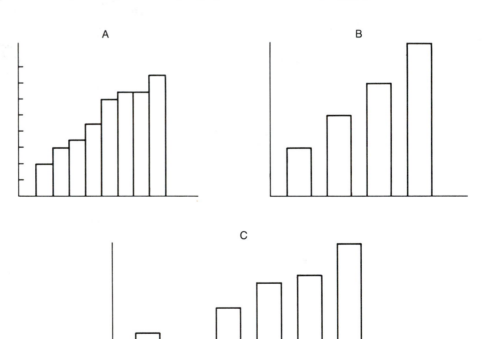

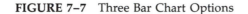

FIGURE 7–7 Three Bar Chart Options

the bars represent. The example in Figure 7–7 includes extra space between the first two bars because the y-axis skips a year for which information was not available.

Bar Chart Rule #4: Arrange bars in an order that best suits your purpose.

Since the reader grasps the bar chart's meaning by comparing bar lengths, you must choose an order that creates impact and, of course, accuracy. Here are three options:

- ○ Sequential—used when the progress of the bars reveals a trend— for example, the increasing number of your company's projects over the last five years.

- ○ Ascending or descending order—used when you want readers to be influenced by the rising or falling of the bars—for example, the five most fuel-efficient bulldozers on the market, placed in ascending order (with your firm's highly efficient bulldozer represented by the last bar).

- ○ Alphabetical—used, as a last resort, when trends are unimportant and thus when no specific order serves your purpose in the chart—for example, economic growth in the seven Maine counties in which you propose building new retail outlets for a hardware store chain.

Bar Chart Rule #5: Be creative by using segmented bars, grouped bars, or other variations.

Figure 7–8 reveals two common techniques for introducing more comparisons into a proposal bar chart. Both the segmented (divided) bars and the grouped bars permit the chart to reflect several different comparisons. Again, remember not to complicate a bar chart so that you obscure the main comparisons.

Five Rules for Line Charts. Perhaps more than any other visual aid, the line chart telegraphs meaning immediately. A line that moves up or down, either gradually or precipitously, can evoke reader response even before the labels are read. With that potential for influence, the line chart is an important part of the proposal writer's persuasive strategy.

Line charts contain vertical and horizontal axes that reflect quantities of two different variables. The vertical or y-axis usually plots the dependent variable; the horizontal or x-axis plots the independent variable. The dependent variable is affected by changes in the independent. Lines then connect the points that have been plotted on the chart. There are five basic rules for planning and drawing line charts in proposals.

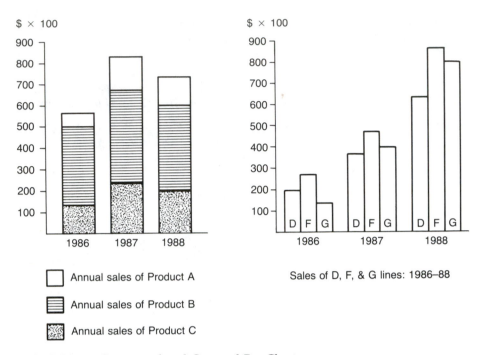

FIGURE 7–8 Segmented and Grouped Bar Charts

Line Chart Rule #1: Use line charts to stress trends.

The direction and angle of the chart's line carry an emotional message to the reader. Exploit this feature in your proposal. For example, assume you are proposing a new medical plan to a firm that has had double-digit increases in its plan costs over the last five years. Your plan guarantees no increases for the next three years. A line chart like the one in Figure 7–9 would create quite an impact on company managers beleaguered by recent increases.

Line Chart Rule #2: Place line charts strategically.

Given their powerful impact, line charts deserve high visibility in your proposal. Here are three good places to put them:

- ○ Title page (to serve as an attention-grabber)
- ○ Beginning of the section describing need (to emphasize the immediacy of a problem)
- ○ Conclusion (to stress a major benefit)

Line Chart Rule #3: Strive for accuracy and clarity.

By virtue of their emotional impact, line charts can be abused in much the same way as bar charts. Specifically, you must make sure you have chosen a

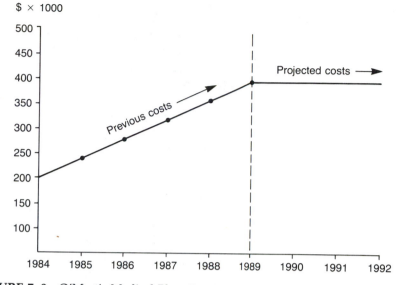

FIGURE 7–9   O'Mart's Medical Plan: Previous vs. Projected Costs

scale that truly reflects the data represented on the chart. Exaggerated changes on line charts are not merely inaccurate; they are unethical. Select a scale that does not mislead the reader with visual tricks. Here are techniques for maintaining both accuracy and visual clarity in line charts:

- Start all scales from zero to eliminate the possible confusion of a "suppressed zero."
- When lack of space requires deleting quantities on either scale, do so in an obvious way. Use parallel lines to break the scale.
- Select a vertical/horizontal axis-length ratio that is pleasing to the eye. A conventional ratio is three to four (that is, the vertical axis measures three-fourths the length of the horizontal). As we have noted, however, the main criterion for scale length is the need for the chart to reflect trends accurately.
- Make lines on the chart itself much thicker than the vertical and horizontal scale lines, to attract the reader's attention.
- Use shading under lines, if this technique increases readability.

> Line Chart Rule #4: Avoid including numbers
> on the line chart itself.

Like bar charts, line charts rely on simplicity for their effect. Inserting numbers on the line itself usually only clutters the clear presentation of the main point—that is, the trend represented by all points on the chart.

Line Chart Rule #5: Use multiple lines with care.

A line chart can, of course, accommodate more than one line. Several lines, as in Figure 7–10, allow you to compare and contrast different trends based on the same two variables. But adding too many divergent lines to the same chart can detract from the immediate impact so apparent in the one-line chart.

A good rule of thumb is to use no more than four or five lines on one line chart. Consider using colors for different lines, but keep in mind that if readers make photocopies of the proposal, the color distinctions on the line chart will not show.

Five Rules for Schedule Charts. Almost every proposal contains a chart that indicates when the proposed activity will be performed—for example, the time needed to deliver a new product or to perform a consulting service. Although the proposal text probably describes the activities in detail, the document also needs an easy-to-read visual aid to summarize the narrative. Schedule charts, which must include dates, are distinguished here from flow charts, which can show the sequence of project activities but usually do not list schedule dates.

Often called Gantt or milestone charts (see Figure 7–11), schedule charts are simple figures that usually include three parts:

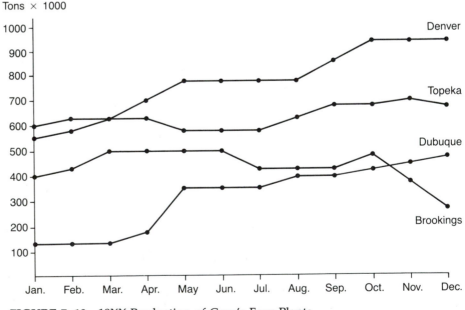

FIGURE 7–10 19XX Production of Gyro's Four Plants

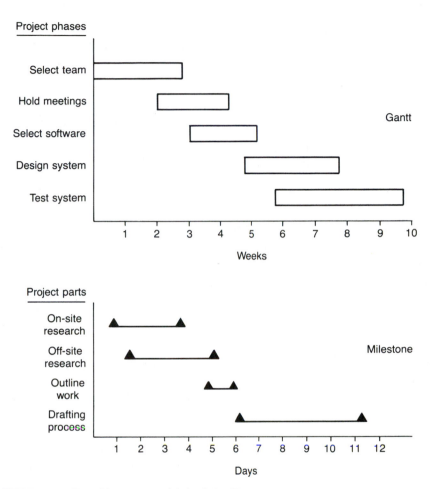

FIGURE 7-11 Two Variations of Schedule Charts

1. A vertical axis that lists the various parts of the project in sequential order
2. A horizontal axis that registers the most appropriate time units
3. Horizontal bar lines (Gantt chart) and/or separate markers (milestone chart) showing the time needed to complete each activity

Five simple guidelines will help you produce schedule charts that are easy for even the most hurried reader to understand.

Schedule Chart Rule #1: Include only main activities.

Focus the reader's eyes on main tasks by avoiding excessive clutter on the vertical axis, which lists events. Ten or fifteen are plenty for one schedule chart. If you must list many more, break them into subactivities to include on additional schedule charts. Carefully and obviously footnote the main schedule chart to indicate where the reader can find the charts with further breakdowns of activities.

Schedule Chart Rule #2: List activities in sequence, starting at the top.

It is conventional to list activities in sequence from the top to the bottom of the vertical axis. The bar arrangement thus allows the reader's eye to move from the top left to the bottom right of the sheet, the most natural reading flow for most people.

Schedule Chart Rule #3: Run all labels in the same direction.

This guideline particularly applies to schedule charts. Their impact should be immediate and clear. If you force readers to turn the page sidewise and then back, they will lose interest in the schedule.

Schedule Chart Rule #4: Invent your own hybrid chart form when appropriate.

Using the milestone and Gantt bar charts as your starting point, you can devise many variations to suit your needs.

Schedule Chart Rule #5: Be realistic in your schedule.

Many proposal writers, in the optimism of the moment, box themselves in with an unrealistic work schedule. Remember that the schedule chart can come back to haunt you. Since the proposal is considered a contract for work, you may be held to the schedule you predict. That fact argues for leaving extra time for activities when possible. Otherwise, you may find yourself requesting schedule changes throughout the course of the project.

Five Rules for Flow Charts. Often misused, this visual aid requires great care in preparation. A flow chart comprises boxes or other shapes connected by arrows, which aim to tell the reader a short story about a process (see Figure 7–12). Too many flow charts become novels instead of short stories. Their job is to simplify the narrative that occurs in the text, not duplicate its complexity. More than any other visual aid, this type demands that you subscribe to the famous KISS principle: "Keep It Short and Simple."

Use proposal flow charts mainly to show the steps for completing whatever change you are suggesting; for example, adding a new product to a firm's clothing line, completing a soil survey before construction begins on a new high-rise, or adding a new employee to your department's support staff.

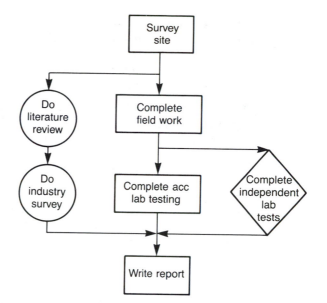

FIGURE 7–12 ACC's Plan for Survey Project

Flow charts permit a good deal of design flexibility, which is one reason they often end up so complicated that they put readers off.

Flow Chart Rule #1: Present only overviews.

Readers look to the flow chart for the "big picture." Give it to them. Reserve intricate detail for listings within the text or in appendices, where readers expect it. This rule means that the flow chart should visually emphasize one main process path.

Flow Chart Rule #2: Use as few different-size shapes as possible.

Most flow charts start with the box or rectangle to represent parts of the process. Introduce other shapes only if additions can be justified by the complexity of the activity. In other words, adding shapes is a trade-off: the flow chart becomes more thorough and specific, but it also becomes more difficult to read quickly. Seek the right balance to accomplish your goal.

Flow Chart Rule #3: Provide a legend that identifies the meaning of different shapes.

Many flow charts assume the reader knows what the shapes mean, perhaps because the proposal narrative describes the process in detail. Readers often look at the flow chart before they read the text, however, so the legend must be in an obvious spot, surrounded by some white space to attract the eye. Legends must list all shapes and their meanings.

Flow Chart Rule #4: Start arrows from top to bottom or from left to right.

These directions correspond to the movement of the reader's eyes. Longer flow charts, of course, may extend beyond one sweep across or down the page. In that case, keep the main direction either vertical or horizontal.

Flow Chart Rule #5: Label all shapes clearly.

Besides the legend that defines the meanings of different shapes, the flow chart must include a label for each square, rectangle, circle, and so forth. If the item is not important enough to label, it is not important enough to be placed on the flow chart. The three main options for labeling are listed in descending order of preference (from the reader's perspective):

1. Place the label inside the shape when space permits.
2. Place the label immediately outside the shape, if this style does not make the flow chart too cluttered.
3. Put a number in each shape, along with a list of number/label correspondences at the bottom of the chart or on another page.

Again, the best flow charts present simplified overviews. Labels inside shapes accomplish this objective. Labels outside shapes move the reader's eye away from the flow. And labels at the bottom of the page or on another page place an obstacle between the reader and the illustration.

Five Rules for Organization Charts. A mainstay of sales proposals, an organization chart shows relationships among positions, departments, or responsibilities in an organization. On the surface, this would seem to be one of the easiest, least creative visual aids to produce. Such is not the case, however, because the chart in a proposal must be designed to persuade, not merely to describe.

Organization Chart Rule #1: Use the boxes-and-connecting-lines approach to emphasize higher-level positions.

This standard format uses rectangles, and occasionally other geometric shapes, to represent selected positions within the company (see Figure 7–13). Higher positions appear at the top of the page in larger boxes. This approach consequently focuses more visual attention to those higher up in the organization.

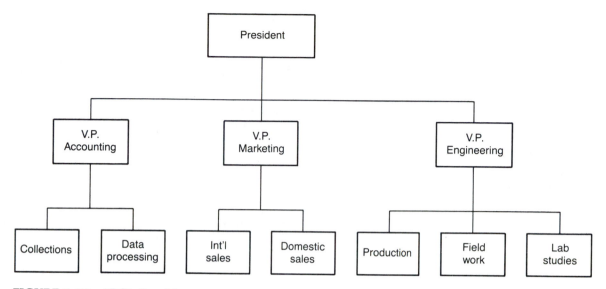

FIGURE 7–13   ABC's Top Management

Organization Chart Rule #2: Use the concentric circles
approach to emphasize middle- and lower-level positions.

This type of organization chart gives more visibility to nonmanagement workers—those who may be most deeply involved in a proposed project. In Figure 7–14, for example, the project engineers are perched on the chart's outer ring. The structure reflects their importance to the project, while still clearly linking them to the umbrella management structure within the company.

Organization Chart Rule #3: Connect
all boxes with solid or dotted lines.

Solid lines reflect direct reporting relationships within the company and run vertically when the chart moves from the top to the bottom of the page. When organization charts are drawn from left to right across the page, the solid lines for reporting relationships run horizontally.

Dotted lines reflect staffing relationships, that is, positions that provide support for another person but do not report directly to her or him. These lines usually go out at right angles from the main direction of the chart. Be careful not to include too many dotted-line relationships, since a chart with too many staff lines looks cluttered and makes company work appear disorganized.

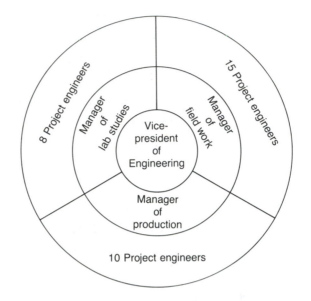

FIGURE 7–14 Staff Available for HDO Project

Organization Chart Rule #4: Use varied shapes judiciously.

As with flow charts, you can introduce different shapes on an organization chart to represent different levels or types of jobs. But be aware of the trade-off: readers will be able to identify certain positions by the shape used on the chart, but the chart as a whole will become "busier." Use more than one shape only if you are convinced the trade-off works to the readers' benefit.

Organization Chart Rule #5: Be creative.

When standard forms won't work, use your imagination to create new ones. Unlike most other types of visuals, organization charts leave a good deal of room for individual design to suit your purpose. In Figure 7–15, for example, sunlight-type rays emanate from the project-director box to show the lines of responsibility in the project, yet the standard reporting and staffing lines remain as another level of meaning.

Five Rules for Tables.   Tables present the reader with raw data (usually numbers) that would otherwise clutter the text of a proposal. They are grouped separately from other visual aids because they elicit quite a different response from readers: they present statistical information that the reader must then interpret. By virtue of their fairly standard form, tables fail to produce the emotional impact of charts. Instead, they must rely on clarity of presentation for their effect.

Tables are sometimes classified as either formal or informal; the formal

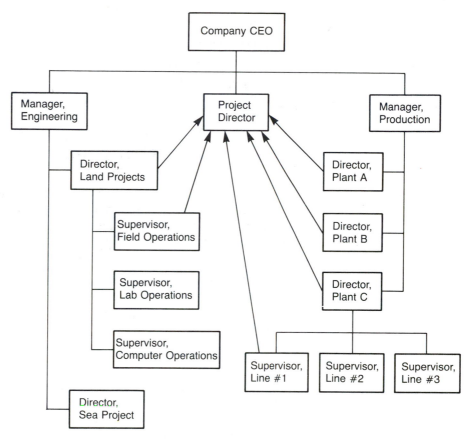

FIGURE 7–15 Main Reporting Lines: Proposed Jaycore Project

type is more complex and much more common. Formal tables present data by means of a grid, always with both horizontal rows and vertical columns. Informal tables present data in the form of either rows or columns.

Table Rule #1: Use informal tables as extensions of the text rather than as separate graphics.

Their simple content permits a simple format. Instead of shifting to a new page, as you would with a formal table, merge the informal table into your paragraph; for example:

By the end of last month, we had shipped 22 new units to our offices in New York State. As shown below, most units went to Buffalo:

Buffalo Office	15 Units
Albany Office	4 Units
Potsdam Office	3 Units

As part of the text, the informal table usually has these features:

- No table number or title
- No previous reference in text
- No listing in List of Illustrations

Relegate information to an informal table only when justified by sparse content.

Table Rule #2: Use formal tables for data that you can afford to separate from text.

Formal tables usually appear on the page following the first text reference. If they present less important information, they can also be placed in an appendix. In either case, the reader must make an effort to locate the table and extract the information before returning to the text. These facts suggest that you should

- Highlight important data by noting them in the text as well as in the table
- Make every table as clear and visually inviting as possible

Table Rule #3: Create appealing tables by using plenty of white space both around and within them.

When used effectively, white space guides the eye through a table much better than do black lines. Avoid putting boxes around tables; instead, leave an extra inch or so of white space than you would normally leave around text. This guideline applies to informal tables that are merged with text and to formal tables that appear on separate pages.

Also, avoid horizontal and vertical lines between rows and columns. Instead use just enough space to attract the reader's eye and to provide adequate breaks among the data. Can you use too much white space? Yes, if the reader has trouble following along rows or columns. Design the right balance into each table.

Table Rule #4: Follow the usual conventions for dividing and explaining data in formal tables.

Figure 7–16 shows the form that most readers expect of a formal table. Follow these basic structural guidelines in creating tables:

1. Number tables if the proposal contains more than one.
2. List table numbers and titles in the list of illustrations (in a formal proposal).
3. Give titles to all formal tables, and place them, with the number, above the table.

No. **1345.** DOMESTIC PERSONAL COMPUTER SALES AND USE: 1981 TO 1985

ITEM	Unit	1981	1982	1983	1984	1985
Personal computers sold	Mil. units	1.11	3.53	6.90	7.70	7.10
Value	Bil. dol.	3.14	5.93	9.79	14.49	18.20
Personal computers in use, total [1]	**Mil. units**	**2.12**	**5.53**	**12.17**	**19.39**	**25.87**
Workplace	Mil. units	1.24	2.26	4.00	6.47	9.46
Business: 1–49 employees	Mil. units	.30	.55	.99	1.68	2.56
50–999 employees	Mil. units	.24	.44	.77	1.24	1.85
Over 999 employees	Mil. units	.47	.88	1.61	2.64	3.78
Government	Mil. units	.24	.40	.62	.91	1.27
Education	Mil. units	.13	.27	.54	.94	1.45
Kindergarten through grade 12	Mil. units	.10	.21	.40	.70	1.09
College/university	Mil. units	.03	.06	.14	.24	.36
Homes	Mil. units	.75	3.00	7.64	11.99	14.96
Personal computer-related equipment in use:						
Impact printers	Mil. units	.72	1.90	4.25	8.68	13.11
Nonimpact printers	Mil. units	.02	.10	.31	.67	1.25
Plotters	Mil. units	.02	.05	.12	.24	.45
Monochrome monitors	Mil. units	.97	2.24	4.68	8.19	12.06
Color monitors	Mil. units	.13	.48	1.29	2.79	5.03
Modems	Mil. units	.18	.53	1.41	3.02	5.07
Add-in-boards [2]	Mil. units	2.41	5.68	11.43	19.50	30.69

[1] Excluding multiuser personal computers.   [2] Excluding add-in modem boards.

Source: Future Computing, Inc., Dallas, TX, unpublished data.

FIGURE 7–16 Example of Formal Table

4. Create short but clear headings for all columns and rows.

5. Include in headings any necessary abbreviations or symbols, such as lb. or %.

6. Round off numbers as much as possible, for ease of reading, and line up multidigit numbers to the right edge.

7. Place brief explanatory headnotes between the title and the table.

8. Place brief explanatory footnotes below the table.

9. Place any necessary source references below the footnotes.

10. Use upper- and lowercase letters rather than full caps.

11. Spell out abbreviations and define terms in a key or footnote if *any* reader may need such help.

12. Make each table absolutely self-contained and clear.

Table Rule #5: Usually, put cost information in tables.

We saw in Chapter 4 that costs should sometimes be buffered by presenting their rationale first—a good persuasive strategy. When you get to the numbers, however, put them clearly before the reader in informal or formal tables, depending upon their complexity.

The reason for putting costs in tables is simple. Readers should not have to dig through paragraphs of narrative to find out what the project will cost. A frustrating search may lead to suspicions that you are trying to bury cost information. It is better to face costs head-on by placing them in clear, well-labeled tables.

SUMMARY

Graphics (also called *illustrations* or *visual aids*) help make a proposal come alive for the reader. They come in the form of tables (rows and columns of data) and figures (an umbrella term for all graphics other than tables). Although most proposal readers want some graphics, the trick is to discover the particular ones your readers favor. Do some research to learn their preferences. Whatever graphics you select, remember the three main reasons for using them: to simplify ideas, to reinforce ideas, and to stimulate interest. The seven types of visual aids often used in proposals are pie charts, bar charts, line charts, schedule charts, flow charts, organization charts, and tables.

These basic rules apply to all visuals:

1. Refer to all graphics in the text
2. Place graphics immediately after the first text reference to them
3. Try to arrange graphics so they can be read without turning the proposal sidewise
4. Avoid clutter
5. Provide adequate titles, notes, keys, and source data

EXERCISES

1. *Pie, bar, and line charts*

   Complete this exercise using the data in Table 7-1 and the appropriate guidelines in this chapter. The table shows total U.S. energy production and consumption from 1960 to 1985. It also breaks down production and consumption into four main groupings.

   a. Construct a pie chart that reflects the four groupings of percentage breakdowns for U.S. energy consumption in 1980.

   b. Construct a grouped bar chart (see Bar Chart Rule #5) that reflects both U.S. total production and U.S. total consumption figures for 1960, 1965, 1970, 1975, 1980, and 1985.

   c. Construct a line chart that reflects the trend in U.S. total energy consumption from 1970 through 1979.

2. *Schedule charts*

   a. Construct a horizontal bar schedule chart to reflect your work on a past, present, or future writing project.

TABLE 7–1 Energy Production and Consumption, by Major Source: 1960 to 1985

[Btu=British thermal unit. For Btu conversion factors, see text, section 19. See also *Historical Statistics, Colonial Times to 1970*, series M 76–92]

YEAR	Total production (quad. Btu)	PERCENT OF PRODUCTION				Total consumption (quad. Btu)	PERCENT OF CONSUMPTION				Consumption/ production ratio
		Coal	Petroleum [1]	Natural gas [2]	Other [3]		Coal	Petroleum [1]	Natural gas [2]	Other [3]	
1960	41.5	26.1	36.0	34.0	3.9	43.8	22.5	45.5	28.3	3.8	1.06
1961	42.0	24.9	36.2	34.9	4.0	44.5	21.6	45.5	29.1	3.8	1.06
1962	43.6	25.0	35.6	35.1	4.2	46.5	21.3	45.2	29.5	4.0	1.07
1963	45.9	25.8	34.8	35.4	4.0	48.3	21.5	44.9	29.8	3.7	1.05
1964	47.7	26.2	33.9	35.8	4.0	50.5	21.7	44.2	30.3	3.8	1.06
1965	49.3	26.5	33.5	35.8	4.3	52.7	22.0	44.1	29.9	4.0	1.07
1966	52.2	25.8	33.7	36.4	4.1	55.7	21.8	43.8	30.5	3.8	1.07
1967	55.0	25.1	33.9	36.5	4.4	57.6	20.7	43.9	31.2	4.2	1.05
1968	56.8	24.0	34.0	37.6	4.4	61.0	20.2	44.2	31.5	4.1	1.07
1969	59.1	23.5	33.1	38.7	4.8	64.2	19.3	44.1	32.2	4.4	1.09
1970	62.1	23.5	32.9	38.9	4.7	66.4	18.5	44.4	32.8	4.3	1.07
1971	61.3	21.5	32.7	40.5	5.3	67.9	17.1	45.0	33.1	4.8	1.11
1972	62.4	22.6	32.1	39.7	5.6	71.3	16.9	46.2	31.9	5.0	1.14
1973	62.1	22.5	31.4	39.9	6.2	74.3	17.5	46.9	30.3	5.3	1.20
1974	60.8	23.1	30.5	38.9	7.4	72.5	17.5	46.1	30.0	6.5	1.19
1975	59.9	25.0	29.6	36.8	8.6	70.5	17.9	46.4	28.3	7.4	1.18
1976	59.9	26.1	28.8	36.4	8.6	74.4	18.3	47.3	27.4	7.1	1.24
1977	60.2	26.2	29.0	36.4	8.5	76.3	18.2	48.7	26.1	7.0	1.27
1978	61.1	24.4	30.2	35.6	9.9	78.1	17.6	48.6	25.6	8.1	1.28
1979	63.8	27.5	28.4	35.0	9.1	78.9	19.1	47.1	26.2	7.7	1.24
1980	64.8	28.7	28.2	34.2	8.9	76.0	20.3	45.0	26.8	7.8	1.17
1981	64.4	28.5	28.2	34.2	9.1	74.0	21.5	43.2	26.9	8.4	1.15
1982	63.9	29.2	28.7	32.0	10.2	70.8	21.6	42.7	26.1	9.6	1.11
1983	61.2	28.2	30.1	30.6	11.2	70.5	22.6	42.6	24.6	10.2	1.15
1984	65.9	30.0	28.6	30.7	10.7	74.1	23.0	41.9	25.0	10.1	1.13
1985, prel	64.7	30.0	29.2	29.6	11.3	73.8	23.7	41.8	24.1	10.5	1.14

[1] Production includes crude oil and lease condensate. Consumption includes domestically produced crude oil, natural gas liquids, and lease condensate, plus imported crude oil and products. [2] Production includes natural gas liquids; consumption excludes natural gas liquids. [3] Comprised of hydropower, nuclear power, geothermal energy and other.

Source: U.S. Energy Information Administration, *Annual Energy Review.*

b. Select a technical project that you plan to complete on the job or in a course. Construct a milestone schedule chart that shows some or all of the proposed activities.

3. *Flow charts*

Using the flow chart rules in this chapter, construct a flow chart that describes a process with which you are familiar. For example, you may want to base your chart on schedule information mentioned in the previous exercise.

4. *Organization charts*

a. Create an organization chart with concentric circles. Use personnel data from your own work experience, from interviews with members of other organizations, or from library research about companies.

b. Create a conventional organization chart with geometric shapes. Use personnel data from your college, from your employer, or from your research into the structure of other organizations.

5. *Table and figure from same data*

Use the guidelines in this chapter to construct a formal table that includes all data in the following fictional case; then create one figure that highlights some of the data in your table.

Your table is meant to show the significant sales increases in six main food products of your firm, Tasty Foods, Inc. You also want this table to reflect the increased percentage of product sales being exported. The six products are diverse, so some kind of grouping will be appropriate on the table. The time frame will be 1986 through 1988. Your best selling product, Basetone Beer, zoomed from 23, to 34, and then to 43 million in sales in the three years. Another big seller was Castle Cake Mix, with three-year sales figures of 18, 19, and 21 million. Both Basetone Beer and Castle Cake Mix had the same export percentages of sales: 12%, 18%, and 21% in the three consecutive years. Your Brandy's Brownies, a relatively new entry, had 2, 4.2, and 6 million in sales in the three years, with export percentages of sales starting high (34%) in 1986 and moving to 38% and 41% in the succeeding years. Another new entry, OK Orange Drink, is having a bit harder time in its competitive market: 1986-88 sales were 1.2, 1.3, and 1.35 million, with export percentages of 3%, 6%, and 4%, respectively. Finally, two old reliable products, Gramp's Granola Bars and Tangy Tea, are holding their own. The first went from 21, to 14, and then to 15 million in sales in 1986–88, with export percentages of 32%, 42%, and 42%. Tangy Tea—though with low sales of 3, 4.5, and 6.1 million—had outstanding export percentages of 45%, 59%, and 71% in the three years.

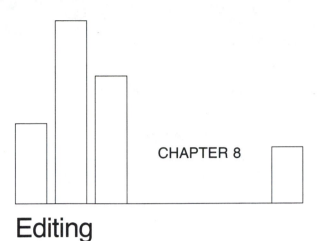

CHAPTER 8

Editing

OBJECTIVES
- ○ Learn more about the editing process
- ○ Learn rules for making stylistic changes
- ○ Learn rules for correcting major grammatical errors
- ○ Learn rules for proofreading for mechanical errors
- ○ Practice editing exercises

In the editing process you should adjust style, grammar, and mechanics to make your writing most persuasive. Except for professional editors, no one likes to do this job. It is a painstaking process that forces you to pick apart your prose, usually when you would much rather get the project out the door. Yet you must persevere! Editing demands the same amount of time and attention as the other two stages of writing—planning and drafting.

Editing Process

The word *process* suggests that you should edit in steps. The quality of the final draft depends on the order and thoroughness of this procedure. We will describe three editing steps and deal with the number of readings, and readers, that may be needed.

Three Steps. As mentioned in Chapter 2, you should follow these basic steps while editing:

Editing Step #1: Refine the style.

Style denotes the personal stamp you give your writing. You can adjust style by changing sentence structure, paragraph length, and word choice, for example.

Editing Step #2: Correct grammar.

Unlike style, which concerns matters of preference or writing options, *grammar* refers to matters of correctness. While editing for grammar, for example, you check for errors in pronoun use, agreement in number between subjects and verbs, and punctuation.

Editing Step #3: Proofread for mechanics.

Mechanics covers errors in spelling, format, and typographical reproduction. Examples are misplacement of decimal points, wrong spacing between letters and lines, misnumbered pages, wrong format for headings, and inconsistent handling of numbers.

Number of Readings. Breaking the editing process into three stages allows you to focus on specific types of errors during a particular reading, rather than trying to make all types of changes during one pass through the document. For example, if you often make subject-verb agreement errors, Step 2 might involve one reading just for agreement and a second reading for all other grammatical errors. Or if you often misspell the same words, and do not have the help of an automatic word processing dictionary, you may read the document three or four times just for mechanics. In other words, read drafts as many times as necessary to ensure flawless copy.

Number of Readers. In editing, too many cooks *won't* spoil the broth. The more sets of eyes that see a document, the better its chances of being edited well. First, ask a superior to read and suggest stylistic changes in a particularly important letter or part of a proposal, such as an executive summary. Give the person a clear idea of the audience and its probable needs. Mention two or three criteria that concern you, such as a benefit-centered tone and easy-to-read paragraphs. Most managers will agree to read selected sections for you; some will even be flattered by your request. Whatever the case, you will receive the benefit of experiences they have gathered in writing similar documents, perhaps to the same audience.

Second, adopt a version of the "buddy system" by asking a colleague to review the draft for grammatical errors after you have done a thorough screening. When that person later writes a proposal or letter, he or she may ask the same favor of you. Another version of the buddy system involves reading aloud to someone else while he or she follows along on another copy of the document. Although this dual reading takes time, it is an excellent way to slow down the editing process so as to catch more errors.

Third, take full advantage of any editing services your firm offers, particularly in the third step of proofreading. If a company proofreader has corrected the document, you may then have only to double-check matters of most concern, such as the correctness of dollar figures in a proposal. Remember, however, that you are ultimately responsible for everything with your name on it, no matter who else may have helped edit, so always make one last pass through any document you sign.

Five Rules for Improving Style

Like fingerprints, writing styles are unique. Throughout your life you have accumulated your own ideas about the way you want to communicate with others on paper. Despite this individuality, however, a few basic rules of style apply to all good writing. The five rules for Step 1 of the editing process are intended to make your proposals and sales letters conversational and persuasive.

Style Rule #1: Be concise without sacrificing clarity.

Long, complicated words and phrases do not impress readers. Outside of Scrabble and crossword puzzles, erudite words (like *erudite*) can only get you in trouble. Particularly in sales writing, you should write as you speak, and most of us speak with a simple and clear vocabulary.

Conciseness in proposals and letters benefits everyone—the reader, you, and your company. It helps the reader, because all readers, especially proposal readers, are impatient to discover what you have to tell them. They will turn off to your ideas quickly if you throw a lot of unnecessary verbiage at them. Careful editing can result in ten to fifteen percent fewer pages and much less frustration for the reader. Conciseness helps you because wordiness sometimes stems from uncertainty or fuzzy thinking. As you work at writing lean prose, you improve your ability to think clearly about the implications of your proposal. And conciseness helps your company because routinely paring down drafts by, say, ten percent greatly reduces typing and printing costs. So conciseness is a worthy goal, but how to achieve it? Here are three techniques.

- ○ Use short words. Never use a long, abstract word when a short, concrete one will do. The words in the left column, for example, can usually be replaced by those in the right column:

advantageous—helpful
alleviate—lessen, lighten
commence—start, begin
discontinue—end, stop
endeavor—try
finalize—end, complete
initiate—start, begin
principal—chief, main
prioritize—rank, rate
procure—buy, get
subsequently—later
terminate—end
utilize—use

○ Shorten wordy phrases, especially trite ones. The culprits here are often long prepositional phrases that seem to do nothing but clutter sentences. Unclutter your writing by finding shorter substitutes, as in these before-and-after examples:

afford an opportunity to—permit
along the lines of—like
an additional—another
at a later date—later
by means of—by
come to an end—end
due to the fact that—because
during the course of—during
give consideration to—consider
in advance of—before
in the final analysis—finally
in the neighborhood of—about
in the proximity of—near

○ Cut clichés from your prose altogether. Most clichés arose as interesting expressions that helped readers see the unknown in terms of the known—a point clear as a piece of crystal ("crystal clear") or costs that accelerate as quickly as a skyrocket ("skyrocketing costs"). Once overworked, however, these phrases no longer inspire new images; they just take up space. Clichés like these should be dropped or replaced with a word or two: a step in the right direction; ballpark figure; by leaps and bounds; efficient and effective; explore every avenue; few and far between; firm but fair; for all intents and purposes; heart of the matter; last but not least;

leaves much to be desired; needless to say; reinvent the wheel; too numerous to mention.

Style Rule #2: Use strong, active-voice verbs.

English verbs are either transitive, intransitive, or linking. *Linking* verbs simply connect subjects with words that rename or modify the subjects. ("George *is* an excellent writer.") *Intransitive* verbs express complete action and thus are not followed by direct objects. ("The word-processing printer *failed.*") *Transitive* verbs transfer action from the subject to the direct object. ("We *will use* a subcontractor's services.")

The terms *active* and *passive* apply only to transitive verbs. When a verb is in the active voice, its subject performs the action. Somebody *does* something, as in "We *will drill* four borings at the site." The emphasis is clearly on the agent of the action. When a verb is in the passive voice, its subject receives the action of the verb, as in "Four borings *will be drilled* by us at the site." Here the emphasis is on the thing being done rather than on the agent. Note that *voice* concerns the perspective from which the sentence is written, not the time (or tense) of the verb phrase.

From the examples, you can see that these predictable changes take place when an active-voice sentence is converted to the passive voice:

The subject becomes the object of a prepositional phrase ("by us") or is dropped from the sentence altogether, possibly making it unclear who completed the action.

The verb phrase is lengthened ("will be drilled" as opposed to "will drill").

The direct object in the active sentence becomes the subject in the passive sentence ("borings").

Thus passive-voice sentences tend to be longer, less forceful, and often less clear as to agents of the action than their active-voice counterparts. Why, then, do writers so often use them? Putting the best face on it, many writers believe the passive voice sounds most "objective" and "scientific." Most readers, on the other hand, tend to view passive-voice writing as boring at best and confusing at worst, for it often fails to say *who* is doing *what*. Style Rule #2 responds to readers' needs by suggesting that most (not all) sentences be phrased in the active voice. Use active verbs when

1. You want to make clear who is responsible for an action ("Mark Swope, a member of our staff, will observe the installation . . .")

2. You want to emphasize a company name—yours or a client's ("Danzell Plastics needs three new extrusion machines for its plant at . . .")

3. You want to replace a top-heavy sentence with one that mentions a table or figure at the beginning ("Figure 1 includes an illustration of the main frame design . . .")

4. You want writing to be as concise as possible (active sentences are by definition shorter than passives)

Use passive verbs when

1. You want to break the monotony of active-voice writing

2. You do not know the agent of the action ("The present machines were installed over thirty years ago . . .")

3. You want to avoid repetitive use of "I" and "we" in passages that require you to state what you will provide, particularly when your first use of the active voice identified "who's going to do what" (also see Style Rule #3)

4. The action is clearly more important than the agent ("Billing statements for the project will be sent at one-month intervals throughout the five-year project . . .")

Style Rule #3: Choose wording that reflects the reader's perspective.

When writing the first draft or two, you naturally tend to present information from your own perspective. The proposal or letter becomes peppered with lots of first-person pronouns and repetitions of your company name (in sales proposals) or department name (in in-house proposals). Fortunately, editing for style gives you the chance to change to the reader's perspective. Specifically, replace first-person pronouns (I, we) with second-person pronouns (you, your) whenever possible. Also, work to subordinate the name of your own firm or department in favor of emphasizing the name of the reader's unit. The principle here is simple: when readers see their own names, they are more likely to believe that you want to identify and meet *their* needs.

Use the following examples and critique as models for applying this rule of style to your own writing:

Example before revision
Mongood Ambulance Conversions, Inc., is pleased to respond to your request for a proposal to provide three new van ambulances to the City of Nickelville, Texas. Mongood has been converting vans of all makes into full-service emergency vehicles for over ten years, and supplied your city with its first van in 19XX. We are certain we can provide a product that will meet the needs of your medical units.

Example after revision
The City of Nickelville, Texas, needs three new van ambulances, as noted in your RFP of May 4, 19XX. You also note that these full-service vehicles must be delivered by October 2, 19XX, in plenty of time for the opening of the new emergency center at Gent Memorial Hospital. In 19XX you purchased your first van ambulance, a Mongood conversion that still serves the City. Now the new demands of Gent Memorial require even more sophisticated vans.

The very first sentence of the unrevised example reveals a greater concern for the writer than for the client. The second and third sentences reinforce this tone by putting more stress on the features of Mongood than on the needs of Nickelville. The revision, on the other hand, starts out with the client's name and the strong verb, "needs." It also acknowledges the very important reason for the October 2, 19XX, delivery deadline—the opening of the new emergency center. Even the reference to the previous purchase is now couched in language that shows the city's needs have changed, despite the good service of the 19XX van. In short, the revised version adopts the reader's perspective.

Style Rule #4: Create parallel form in lists and headings.

Parallel form means simply that like items are phrased in a like manner. Appropriate parallel form allows the reader to move quickly through your proposal, without being slowed by awkward shifts in structure. While editing for parallel form, pay particular attention to headings at the same level and to listings (both in sentences and in indented passages). This example concerns four subheadings of the same heading:

(Before revision)
Subheading A: Surveying High School Principals
Subheading B: Evaluating Survey Results
Subheading C: Petition to Board of Education
Subheading D: Recommending Curriculum Action

(After revision)
Subheading A: Surveying High School Principals
Subheading B: Evaluating Survey Results
Subheading C: Petitioning Board of Education
Subheading D: Recommending Curriculum Action

The unrevised version contains an error in parallel form. The verb *petition* needs to be changed to the noun (gerund) *petitioning*, to match the other three lead-off words. The next example shows the care with which you must check for parallel form within listings. The closeness of listed items makes the error quite apparent to discerning readers.

(Before revision)
To assemble necessary information on the three computers, we plan to perform these tasks:

○ Write computer firms to request specifications
○ Read related articles in recent periodicals
○ Equipment demonstrations at local stores
○ Interviews with local salespeople will be conducted

(After revision)
To assemble necessary information on the three computers, we plan to perform these tasks:

○ Write computer firms to request specifications
○ Read related articles in recent periodicals
○ Request equipment demonstrations at local stores
○ Interview some local salespeople

The first two bulleted items on the list indicate that the writer wants to convey action by using verbs like "write" and "read." That makes good sense, but the last two items switch to a noun phrase and then to a complete sentence. These errors in parallelism can be corrected by making the third and fourth items start with the verbs *request* and *interview.*

Style Rule #5: Vary length and style of paragraphs and sentences.

We have suggested earlier that both letters and proposals should use shorter paragraphs at beginnings and endings. The fact is that you should avoid lengthy paragraphs in *all* parts of the document because many readers will skip them. Yet you also want to avoid the fragmented effect of too many short, staccato paragraphs. Here are some guidelines to use in editing for paragraph style:

○ Provide variety by using paragraphs of different lengths, usually within a range of two to twelve lines.
○ Seek an average paragraph length of around six lines.
○ Begin most paragraphs, particularly longer ones, with the main idea. Never bury an important point in the middle of a paragraph.
○ Use short paragraphs (two to four lines) to emphasize main points or to provide important transitions, since short paragraphs tend to attract attention.
○ Draw attention to groups of similar ideas by using lists signaled by bullets (like those in this list) or numbers (when referring to steps or a sequence).

As you refine your writing skills, you will find yourself making fewer paragraph adjustments at the editing stage; instead, you will have solved such problems while writing drafts. Sentence length and structure, however, are clearly in the province of editing. Follow these guidelines as you edit for sentence style:

- Place the main point near the beginning of most sentences, avoiding long introductory phrases and clauses. Be particularly wary of long passive-voice sentences in which the main verb appears at the end.

- Focus on one main clause in most sentences (a main clause has a subject and verb and can stand by itself). When you start stringing main clauses together with "ands" and "buts," you dilute meaning and lose the reader.

- Put important ideas in short sentences.

- Achieve an average sentence length of about 15 to 18 words for proposals and 12 to 15 words for letters.

Five Rules for Correcting Grammar

For the rest of your working life, you will encounter nit-picking grammarians disguised as company presidents, accountants, engineers, procurement officers, and other professionals—all of whom are likely to read proposals—so you would be wise to edit carefully for errors in grammar. Grammar, for our purposes, concerns the structure of sentences and the correct use of words (sometimes also called *usage*). The suggestions in this section involve matters of error, whereas most of the style rules covered in the previous section involve matters of preference among several options. (We will describe five grammatical errors that occur frequently in sales writing; if you need a more thorough review of all grammatical rules, consult a complete grammar handbook.)

Grammar Rule #1: Make subjects agree with verbs.

As you learned in elementary school, verbs convey action or state of being. Subjects perform the action and thus answer the question "Who or what _____" (with the verb placed in the blank). Plural subjects take plural verbs, and singular subjects take singular verbs. Agreement errors occur when writers mix singular and plural subjects and verbs. The best editing technique for correcting subject-verb agreement errors is to isolate every subject and verb combination in every sentence. This method allows you to move quickly through the document focusing only on subjects and verbs. This procedure also helps you determine the degree to which you have succeeded in choosing strong verbs to convey action in your proposal or letter. Follow these seven guidelines for making verbs agree with subjects:

○ Use a plural verb when subject parts are connected by *and*. ("The transformer and switchbox are to be delivered by July 1." A compound subject, such as "transformer and switchbox," must take the plural form of the verb.)

○ Make the verb agree with the subject nearest the verb when subject parts are connected by *or* or *nor*. ("Neither prices nor a product description is included in the brochure." Or, "Neither a product description nor prices are included in the brochure.")

○ Make the subject agree with the verb even when the subjective complement is a different number. Sometimes called a *predicate noun* or *adjective*, a subjective complement renames or describes the subject and occurs in sentences with linking verbs—*is, are, was, were*, etc. ("The topic of the proposal is windows for the old dormitory." The subject of the sentence, *topic*, is singular, whereas the complement, *windows*, is plural. Thus the verb *is* must be singular to match *topic*.)

○ Use a singular verb even when a singular subject is followed by other nouns in phrases beginning with *as well as, along with*, or *in addition to*. ("The president of the firm as well as the procurement officer is to address the meeting." The sentence subject, "president," is singular and followed by a prepositional phrase. If you were to change *as well as* to *and*, however, the resulting compound subject would require that you change the verb to its plural form, *are*.)

○ Usually use singular verbs with collective nouns. Your choice depends upon the meaning of the collective noun. A collective noun, though singular in form, refers to a group of persons or things *(audience, committee, crowd, family, team, public)*. When a collective noun obviously refers to a group as a whole, use a singular verb. ("The engineering team arrives by helicopter each morning." On the other hand, when the collective noun refers to the members of the group as they act separately, use a plural verb. "The committee do not agree on where to place the rig." If such collective noun–plural verb combinations sound awkward, rephrase the sentence: "The committee *members* do not agree on where to place the rig.")

○ Use a plural verb with irregular plurals such as *data, phenomena, strata*, and *analyses*. The word that seems to pose the most trouble is *data*. Particularly in scientific and engineering writing, most readers expect this generically plural form to take a plural verb. ("The data are to be evaluated by March 15." But if your meaning is singular and you want to avoid the archaic *datum*, rephrase the sentence. "A part of the data is to be evaluated by March 15." Here the subject is the singular *part; data* is only the object of the preposition *of*. Thus the verb must be singular.)

- Use a singular verb with indefinite pronouns such as *all, any, anybody, anyone, each, either, everyone, nobody, none, one, some,* and *someone.* The most prominent exception to this rule is that *all, any,* and *some* may be plural in instances where the meaning is clearly plural. ("Each of the designers is aware of the demands to be placed on the building." "All of the machinists have expressed a preference for the new schedule.")

Grammar Rule #2: Check all pronouns to avoid unclear reference, agreement errors, and sexism.

Pronouns, such as *this, it, he, she,* and *they,* are words that serve in place of nouns. As such, they are convenient for avoiding repetition of the same nouns, but they can also pose problems. These techniques will help you to use pronouns properly.

- Be certain that your writing makes absolutely clear what pronouns like *this* and *that* refer to. Even better, rephrase sentences by turning these vague pronouns into adjectives. (Change "This will be completed by next August" to "This phase of construction will be completed by next August.")

- Check every pronoun for agreement in number with its antecedent (the noun to which it refers). Of special concern are the pronouns *it* and *they.* (Change "General Motors plans to complete their Wyoming plant by next April" to "General Motors plans to complete its Wyoming plant by next April.")

- Never use male pronouns and adjectives, such as *he* and *his,* to represent categories that could include both men and women. Overtly sexist language, though a convention for hundreds of years, gives some readers the impression that only men inhabit the category to which you refer. Speaking more practically, your sales writing may well be read by women professionals who might be offended by your use of masculine pronouns. Avoid the problem by using plural forms or by using the phrases *he or she* or *his or her.* (Change "When a worker enters the site, he should make sure to wear his hardhat" to "When workers enter the site, they should make sure to wear their hardhats.")

Grammar Rule #3: Make all modification clear.

The longer a sentence, the more likely it will contain modifiers (words or groups of words that moderate the meaning of other sentence parts). The two main problems are dangling and misplaced modifiers. When a modifying phrase "dangles," it usually begins or ends a sentence that contains no specific word for it to modify. ("In designing the foundation, several alternatives will be discussed." Who is "designing" here?) When a modifying phrase is misplaced, it seems to refer to a word that it obviously should not modify. ("Floating peacefully near the rig, we saw two humpback whales." The whales were "floating," not the observers, so the sentence must be adjusted.)

At best, dangling or misplaced modifiers produce a momentary misreading or a good laugh; at worst, they can leave the reader hopelessly confused about who is doing what in the sentence. Follow these two strategies to avoid errors:

- Place all modifying phrases as close as possible to the word that they modify. ("Leaving the office on Saturday, we should be able to arrive in Tunis by Monday morning.")
- Correct modification errors, found during the editing process, by reworking the sentence. (Change "Using satellite surveying techniques and several ships, the position can be located by next Tuesday" to "Using satellite surveying techniques and several ships, we can locate the position by next Tuesday" or to "If we use satellite surveying techniques and several ships, the position can be located by next Tuesday.")

Grammar Rule #4: Check all commas.

Most writers have few problems with periods, semicolons, colons, and dashes. Periods end sentences. Semicolons divide short, closely related sentences and separate items in a listing when the items contain intervening commas. Colons announce a formal list and follow statements that introduce explanations. Dashes set off sudden breaks in thought.

Comma use, however, is not as easy to pin down and causes many writers much agony and wasted time. Fortunately, just a few basic rules cover most instances in which commas should be used. Once you learn these basic strategies, editing for grammar will go a good deal faster:

- Use a comma to separate words, clauses, or short phrases written in a series of three or more items. ("The materials will be ordered from Gibson Supply, Wilson Photography, and Davis Wall Products." According to present usage, a comma should always precede the *and* in a series—the so-called serial comma.)

○ Use a comma to separate main clauses joined by coordinate conjunctions such as *and, but, or, nor, so,* and *yet.* ("Many geologic faults may exist at the site, but we have not located any maps that display these faults." Note that the comma is needed because the conjunction "but" separates clauses [groups of words with both a subject and verb]. In the following sentence, there is only one clause and thus no need for a comma: "Many geologic faults may exist at the site but are not displayed on our maps.")

○ Set off nonessential modifiers with commas. A nonessential modifier does not greatly define or limit the word it modifies; it simply adds more information. To put it another way, dropping a nonessential modifier should not greatly affect the central meaning of a sentence. ("The floodplain, which is located about five miles from the site, should not affect our construction plans." Essential modifiers, on the other hand, limit the words they modify and are not enclosed by commas: "The floodplain that is five miles from the site should not affect our construction plans." The implication here is that there may be another floodplain; thus the modifier beginning with *that* is essential in pinpointing a specific floodplain.)

○ Set off nonessential appositives with commas. Appositives expand the meaning of, or rename, the nouns that precede them. The examples include appositives that are nonessential—with commas—and essential—without commas. ("Thomas Perch, author of a book on asbestos, will be one of the investigators." "The word *asbestos* has become associated with major health hazards.")

○ Use a comma to separate two or more coordinate adjectives that modify the same noun. Two tests help to determine if adjacent adjectives are coordinate. First, you should be able to reverse them without a change in meaning. Second, you should be able to substitute *and* for the comma between them. ("They found some black, thick liquid below the tank.")

○ Use a comma after most introductory phrases or clauses that are five words or more. ("Before applying the new salary structure to the other offices, the Human Resources Department should hold meetings with the employees.")

○ Follow conventional usage in placing commas in dates, geographical names, titles, and addresses. ("November 3, 19XX, was the date that Joseph Barnes, Jr., started the firm. Now Barnes, Inc., is a thriving business in eastern Oregon." Note the need for commas after "19XX" and "Inc.")

○ Use commas in lists only if you wish to treat the entire list as a sentence. (Lists in the form of single words or short phrases need not be separated by punctuation.) There are several options for punctuating lists of phrases or clauses. Because lists are often used in proposals, we offer several punctuation options.

"The entire office staff should be able to:

- ○ Respond quickly to customer calls,
- ○ Feed customer complaints to the field staff, and
- ○ Write up each complaint within a day."

Here the nature of the series, with its three phrases, suggests that the list could be treated as a sentence. Depending on your firm's preference, you could also write the list without the commas, without the "and" before the last item, and without the final period. Note that it is customary to capitalize the first word in each item.

As noted earlier, semicolons can be used to separate items in a series when one or more of the items contain commas.

"The entire office staff should be able to:

- ○ Respond quickly to customer calls, as well as to personal visits to the counter;
- ○ Feed customer complaints to the line workers, supervisors, and diggers in the field; and
- ○ Write up each complaint within a day."

The following items are sentences, some of them fairly long. That fact suggests that each be punctuated as a separate sentence, though you would also have the option of using no punctuation.

"We were presented with three alternatives by the consultant:

- ○ The building can be evacuated for three weeks while the sprinklers are installed.
- ○ The workers can move from room to room while the sprinklers are installed section by section.
- ○ The installation can be postponed."

○ Always use a comma when it will clarify meaning, whether or not a rule applies. This commonsense guideline supersedes all others. *Example:* "Any engineer who can, usually presents a paper at the annual conference in Atlanta."

Grammar Rule #5: Avoid common errors in word use.

A few words tend to be wrongly used by many writers. When contained in a proposal or sales letter, this misuse reflects carelessness, at best, and can lead to confusion or even liability problems, at worst. Here are ten words or word pairs that need special attention:

- *affect/effect*: *Affect* is usually a verb meaning "to influence." *Effect* is usually a noun meaning "result." (*Effect* can also be used as a verb meaning "to bring about," but this usage often results in wordiness and should be avoided.)

  "The hurricane did not *affect* his schedule."
  "The *effects* of the hurricane were significant."
  "The treasurer *changed* [not "effected a change in"] the company's check-cashing policy."

- *assure/insure/ensure*: *Assure* means "to promise" and is used in reference to people. *Ensure* and *insure* can be synonyms that mean "make certain"; however, current preference is for *ensure*, reserving the word *insure* for the context of insurance.
  Assure and *ensure* should be used with care in proposals, for they express a degree of absolute promise and certainty to which a writer or company could be held.

  "Be *assured* that the machinery will be delivered by June 1."
  "He will call to *ensure* that the delivery was made."
  "Our agent has agreed to *insure* us adequately for the job."

- *complement/compliment*: As a verb, *complement* means "to add to, to make complete, to reinforce." As a noun, it means "that which completes the whole." *Compliment* is a verb meaning "to flatter" or a noun meaning "flattery." As for adjective forms, *complimentary* means "free" or "related to flattery," whereas *complementary* means "that which adds to, makes complete, or reinforces."

  "The new landscaping will *complement* the building's facade."
  "The *complement* of six recruiters brought the department's staff up to its normal level."
  "The cash award to Jamie was the firm's *compliment* for his solid service."
  "The bidding firms were discouraged from sending *complimentary* gifts at Christmas."

- *compose/comprise*: *Compose* means "to make up" or "to be included in." *Comprise* means "to include" or "to consist of." In other words, the parts *compose* the whole, whereas the whole *comprises* the parts. The phrase *is comprised of* is unacceptable usage and probably results from a corruption of the correct *is composed of*.

  "The technical, management, and cost sections *compose* the proposal."
  "The proposal *comprises* three main sections on technical data, management information, and costs."

○ *continual(ly)/continuous(ly):* These words have quite distinct meanings. *Continual* means "happening over and over, repeatedly," whereas *continuous* means "uninterrupted." Like some other words in this list, this pair must be used with great care in documents (such as proposals) in which misunderstanding can be disastrous.

"Over a three-week period, they will *continually* visit the site to observe the progress of construction."
"Once at the site, our engineer *continuously* observed the grading operation for two hours."
(This usage suggests that she didn't take her eyes off the grading process for two full hours.)

○ *disinterested/uninterested: Disinterested* means "unbiased, impartial." *Uninterested* means simply "not interested." Given the great difference in meaning, don't confuse a reader by using *disinterested* when you mean "not interested."

"We will seek a *disinterested* party to evaluate the progress of the project and mediate the talks between workers."
"They were *uninterested* in responding to the RFP because of the potential liability problems."

○ *farther/further: Farther* refers to physical distance; *further* refers to abstract or metaphorical distance.

"The entire crew had to walk another three miles *farther* before locating the half-buried wreckage."
"After he left, we worked even *further* into the night on the cost projections."

○ *hopefully:* Use this word to mean "in a hopeful way" or "with hope." Do not use it as a substitute for "I hope" or "it is hoped that."

"The proposal team waited *hopefully* for the client's phone call."
"I *hope* that [not 'Hopefully'] the client will call soon."

○ *imply/infer:* The easiest way to distinguish these words is to remember that the speaker or writer *implies* ("suggests"), whereas the listener or reader *infers* ("concludes"). This distinction also applies to the noun derivatives, *implication* and *inference.*

"He *implied* that the firm would probably give us the contract."
"We *inferred* from his remarks that the contract would create some massive scheduling problems."

○ *principal/principle: Principal* as a noun means "head official" or "money on which interest is earned"; as an adjective it means "main, chief, major." This word is often confused with *principle,* a noun meaning "a basic truth or belief."

"The firm assured the clients that one of its *principals,* Mr. James Fedderman, would be involved with the project."
"They planned to pay off the *principal* on the loan."
"The *principal* reason for bidding on that project is the experience it would provide."
"He considered it a violation of his *principles* to work for firms that had been indicted."

Five Rules for Proofreading

This final editing stage, which concerns correctness in spelling, typographical form, and similar mechanical matters, is best done with the help of people who are distanced from the project. One major proofreading problem, spelling, is not dealt with here. We assume that you will scrutinize your proposals and letters for misspelled words. Virtually every person to whom you write expects flawless spelling; it's as simple as that. Besides checking and rechecking for correct spelling, then, here are five important guidelines for proofreading.

Proofreading Rule #1: Check the table of contents for accuracy.

First, make sure the page numbers for sections and subsections correspond to the actual text pages where these sections and subsections begin. Second, check that the table of contents contains all the headings and subheadings in the text, in their proper relationship to each other.

Proofreading Rule #2: Check all dollar figures.

Numbers are difficult to proofread and tend to be given too little attention. This is particularly unfortunate with regard to costs, since an error here can be embarrassing and possibly even ruinous. (Remember that proposals can be considered contracts.) Check every single cost figure, making sure that totals are correct. Unless the client says otherwise, avoid using the decimal points and the accompanying cents figures, because the additional detail invites more mistakes and makes the cost estimates look higher than they are.

Proofreading Rule #3: Check all tables and figures.

First, do as you did with the table of contents—make sure that the list of illustrations contains accurate page references. Second, make sure that your letters and proposals contain references to the correct table and figure numbers. As noted in Chapter 7, these references usually appear on the page before the table or figure. Third, make sure that the reproduction or binding process has not hampered the effectiveness of the graphics.

Proofreading Rule #4: Check all abbreviations.

Obviously, readers need to understand any abbreviations used in the letter or proposal.

- Terms used just a few times should be written out rather than abbreviated, particularly if you are not sure the reader will understand them.
- A term used often in the text should be written out the first time it appears, with the abbreviation following it in parentheses. Then use the abbreviation by itself in later references. In long documents with many pages between uses of an abbreviation, it may be preferable to write out the term every time it appears.
- In a document that uses many abbreviated terms, a glossary of terms at the beginning of the document provides easy reference.

Proofreading Rule #5: Check the form of all numbers.

There are no absolute, hard-and-fast guidelines for writing numbers. Your company, client, or professional society may have its own standards for expressing numbers as either figures (92) or words (ninety-two). If not, here are some common guidelines used by many writers:

- Generally, use figures for numbers of 10 or more and words for numbers less than 10, with exceptions as noted below.
- Do not begin a sentence with a number figure. ("Twenty-five salespersons attended the workshop." "There were 25 salespersons at the workshop.")
- Use number figures to identify graphics. ("See Table 4.")
- Use number figures when a sentence or paragraph contains several closely related numbers, even though some may be less than 10. ("They hired 16 engineers, 5 secretaries, and 3 clerks.")
- When two numbers appear in succession in a phrase other than a series, write one as a word and the other as a figure. ("The crew consisted of 12 six-person teams.")
- Follow a number in words with its corresponding figure in parentheses only in legal documents. ("The hourly rate will be fifty-five dollars [$55].")
- In dollar figures, include cents figures only when exactness to the cent is necessary. (See Proofreading Rule #2.)
- Place commas in figures of five or more digits. ("The project will last 10,000 hours.")

SUMMARY

Editing requires the same effort as the other stages of writing. You achieve the best results by reading a document several times, looking for selected kinds of errors on each pass. Also, seek the help of others during the editing process; the more sets of eyes that edit your writing, the better the chance that all errors will be caught. Careful editing requires that you attend to matters of style, grammar, and proofreading.

Style

1. Be concise without sacrificing clarity
2. Use strong, active-voice verbs
3. Choose wording that reflects the reader's perspective
4. Create parallel form in lists and headings
5. Vary length and style of paragraphs and sentences

Grammar

1. Make subjects agree with verbs
2. Check all pronouns to avoid unclear reference, agreement errors, and sexism
3. Make all modification clear
4. Check all commas
5. Avoid common errors in word use

Proofreading

1. Check the table of contents for accuracy
2. Check all dollar figures
3. Check all tables and figures
4. Check all abbreviations
5. Check the form of all numbers

EXERCISES

1. *Sentences with style errors*

   Revise these sentences by following the style rules in this chapter. Some revisions may need to contain more than one sentence.

   a. The conference last week in downtown Boston afforded us the opportunity to meet with several members of your staff in an effort to make plans to finalize the agreement between our respective firms.

b. Due to the fact that the request for proposal addresses the concerns that we have explored with your department chiefs on occasions too numerous to mention, it is our opinion that a meeting before the proposal is submitted might be the most efficient and effective way of exploring our mutual concerns and thereby discovering the various needs that you want covered in the document, and of arriving at a ballpark figure for the project cost figures.

c. It has become apparent that the above date is not a convenient time for the three firms to hold their joint discussions and it is therefore requested by our firm that another date be established so that the subcontracting discussions can be held in the very near future.

d. A series of step-by-step procedures, which have been established by our field technicians, are certain to give a great deal of assurance that the field work will be accomplished with the necessary accuracy, and the main ones are as follows:

    ○ All samples will be taken from the ground without being disturbed

    ○ Place the samples in plastic bags

    ○ Label bags

    ○ Bags containing the samples will be immediately sent to our Seattle lab for testing

e. In regard to your kind inquiry regarding the availability of our new pump in the Upper Peninsula, it is our pleasant task to inform you that the new pump is carried by two different dealerships, one in the city of Manistique and the other dealer is in the city of Houghton.

f. We are pleased to submit our proposal for the Tri-City construction project that we hope to complete for your firm, Jones Engineering, in 19XX and that we think will satisfy all needs we understood from the project description we recently received at our main office.

g. Conducted under the sponsorship of your firm and our own, the survey that was completed yielded results, as can be seen in Figure 8, that allowed us to prioritize the needs of the managers of all utility firms in the Chicago area.

h. A good deal of care will be utilized by us in determining the most advantageous design for the building referenced in your letter of July 21.

i. It was noted by this writer that several vats of pellets, as a viable alternative, could be shifted to the other production line, as can be seen in the diagram contained in Figure 4.

j. In the neighborhood of about 400 hours were spent by our road crews in an effort to repair the stretch of Route 45, but we are not yet in the position to give our exact determination of the manner in which this amount of time can be effectively reduced on the next repair project.

2. *Sentences with grammar errors*

Revise these sentences by following this chapter's grammar rules. Be able to explain the rationale for each change that you make.

a. His main concern is that the graph, when completed will include all data that was collected at the site.

b. The group from the three mid-town companies are planning another meeting.

c. Cabot Engineering, Inc. announced in their company newsletter that each department supervisor must submit his annual report by next Tuesday.

d. Barry Shockley author of the study, along with his colleague Keven Black are planning to contribute to the project.

e. Because they could not agree on the purchase the three partners decided to seek outside advice.

f. I submitted a thorough well-edited report before the deadline and I was convinced my boss would like it.

g. The plan unless we have completely misjudged it will increase sales markedly.

h. The new personnel database will help us to:

   o Control costs of healthcare;

   o Monitor the training our employees receive;

   o Complete Affirmative Action reports.

i. Each of the proposal coordinators selected their own team for the in-house competition.

j. Either the staff accountants or the office manager are planning to review the cost proposal.

3. *Sentences concerning word use*

   Select the correct word in parentheses and be able to defend your choice.

   a. The decision the president makes next week will be (effected/affected) by the many conversations he has with his managers this week.

   b. He wants to (assure/ensure) that the proposal responds to the client's needs.

   c. To (ensure/insure) that our liability will be limited, we (insured/ensured) the machine for $10,000.

   d. The advertising agency regularly sends out (complementary/complimentary) gifts to all its clients.

   e. The company library (is comprised of/comprises) over 5,000 books. Surprisingly, almost 4,000 of them (compose/comprise) the country's largest collection on geological fault zones.

   f. She (continually/continuously) worked on the tables and figures for several days, stopping only for meetings with the drafters and computer graphics specialists.

   g. After working four years on just one building design, she became (disinterested/uninterested) in the project.

   h. He planned to read (farther/further) after taking a break for lunch.

   i. John had tried to (imply/infer) in his speech that salary raises would be low, but his staff did not receive that (inference/implication).

   j. His (principal/principle) concern was that the loan's interest and (principle/principal) remain under $50,000.

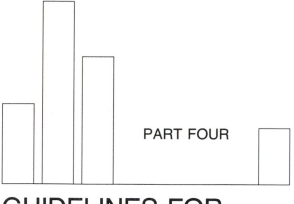

PART FOUR

GUIDELINES FOR SPEAKING

There is more to the proposal process than productive *writing*. Proposals also depend for their success on productive *talking*, sometimes called "interpersonal communication." Talking occurs first among those who plan and write the proposal, since proposals often rely on group efforts, but most talking takes place between you and the decision makers who will act on what you've proposed.

You probably associate the word *performing* with artificial, larger-than-life situations like plays and concerts. Yet that's exactly the way you must view most presentations, meetings, and negotiations with decision makers. Performing does *not* mean "phony"—you must always be genuine. But to get results you must act in a more self-aware, vigorous, and responsive fashion than you do during routine exchanges. In short, you have to be "on" when talking with those who will decide your

proposal's fate.

Chapter 9 concerns opportunities for oral presentations. Like most people, you probably question the use of the word "opportunity" in this context. Few professionals really enjoy preparing for and delivering presentations to managers or clients. But if you can master this challenging part of the proposal process, you will be way ahead of the competition. The guidelines in Chapter 9 focus on delivery, content, and visuals.

Chapter 10 gives pointers for effective meetings and negotiations. Everyone complains about meetings, so you would be wise to train yourself to be a good leader and participant. The last part of Chapter 10 offers suggestions for improving the negotiation process. These guidelines reinforce the main theme of this book: your goal is to build long-term relationships.

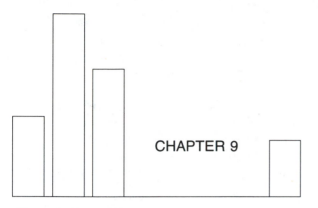

CHAPTER 9

Oral Presentations

Myth has it that public speaking is a God-given talent. If you don't have it, so goes the myth, there's not much you can do to change the situation. This kind of thinking keeps students and professionals from reaching their full potential as speakers. This chapter debunks the "either-you-have-it-or-you-don't" myth. Anyone can become a good, even excellent, speaker by following three steps:

1. Prepare well
2. Practice often
3. Perform vigorously

Conversely, most mediocre or poor presentations result from poor preparation, little practice, and a lackluster performance.

Definition and Use

Sooner or later, most written proposals require a follow-up presentation in person. For sales proposals, clients may ask for a summary of technical, management, and cost information. For in-house proposals, your boss may ask you to highlight the benefits of your idea before a committee of decision makers. Oral presentations on your proposals can vary considerably in four respects:

- ○ Format—from informal question/answer sessions to formal speeches
- ○ Length—from five-minute overviews to exhaustive sessions of an hour or more
- ○ Number of presenters—from solo performances to group presentations by proposal teams
- ○ Content—from brief highlights to intensive examinations of the written proposal

These variables mean that one cardinal rule applies to oral presentations: find out what listeners expect. You need to know their preferences for format, length, number of presenters, and content *before* you invest any time in preparing the presentation.

Once you know what type of presentation is expected, how do you prepare? At this point many people fail to show the same concern for strategy that they showed while preparing the written proposal. This chapter offers guidelines for both the novice who needs a starting point and the experienced speaker who needs only a refresher. The first ten guidelines cover rules for preparing and delivering the text of a speech, and the second ten guidelines cover rules for using graphics. Although the context in this handbook is proposals, these guidelines can apply to all speaking opportunities.

Ten Guidelines for Preparation and Delivery

In preparing a speech, always keep in mind four problems of listeners.

- ○ They probably don't have your knowledge of the product, service, or idea.
- ○ They have heard so many bad presentations that their expectations for yours are low.
- ○ They tend to daydream.
- ○ They cannot "rewind the tape" to review what you've said.

Given these obstacles, you must prepare and deliver your presentation as if the proposal's acceptance depends on it—and it probably does.

Speech Rule #1: Use the Preacher's Maxim.

This well-known maxim reads, "First you tell 'em what you're gonna tell 'em, then you tell 'em, and then you tell 'em what you told 'em." Why do good speakers follow this plan? Because it gives the speech structure. Obvious beginning, middle, and end sections help keep the listeners oriented. Here's how the maxim should work in practice:

1. Right at the outset, in the first 30 seconds, state (a) the precise purpose of the presentation, no matter how obvious it seems to you, and (b) the main points you will cover. For example, you could say "Today we'd like to stress three main benefits you will derive from a new field safety plan: lower insurance premiums, less lost time from accidents, and fewer employee lawsuits for unsafe job sites."

2. Then methodically cover your main points in the body of the speech, making certain to provide obvious transitions ("Besides lower insurance premiums, a second benefit of the new safety plan will be higher morale . . .").

3. Finally, summarize the talk by again referring to each of the main ideas ("In conclusion, you can benefit from this new plan because . . .").

This approach responds to three features shared by most listeners, whatever their profession or level of education:

○ They need a strong start that grabs their attention and gives them a "road map" for understanding the rest of the speech.

○ They need reminders to keep their attention, both because they can't move back and forth within the speech as they can within a written document and because of the natural tendency to lose concentration.

○ They expect a strong finish that wraps up the speech and draws attention to points the speaker considers most important. People remember first what they heard last.

The selective repetition suggested here ensures that you won't leave your readers behind. If you are worried that better listeners will be put off by repetition, relax. Another feature shared by most listeners is that they appreciate confirmation of the main points they think they heard. Repetition gives them assurance.

Speech Rule #2: Stick to just a few main points.

Some experts say that our short-term memory can hold only five items, plus or minus two. In fact, the closer you stay to groupings of three or four, the better the chance that your points will be remembered. For example, if your written proposal mentions ten main benefits of a new product, the oral presentation should distill this list to the three or four most important features. If you simply must mention all ten to satisfy the listeners' needs, then cluster the ten points into three or four groupings—such as product quality, price, and qualifications.

Speech Rule #3: Put notes on cards or on a single sheet of paper.

Always bring notes with you, even if you have memorized your presentation. It is helpful to have a backup in case you get derailed by interruptions. Also, occasionally glancing down at notes looks more natural than speaking as if the presentation were memorized. Test this principle by observing professional speakers, such as network newscasters. Even when they read copy from teleprompting screens—which is most of the time—they look down at notes so that their performance appears more natural and less intense. Take your cue from these experts.

Some speakers prefer 3" × 5" or 4" × 6" notecards for these reasons:

- They are easy to carry in a coat or shirt pocket.
- They prevent confusion by having room for just one or two points per card.
- They can be held in one hand if you move away from the lectern while speaking.

Other speakers prefer an outline or notes on a single sheet of paper, which shows the entire organization at a glance and leaves hands totally free for gestures. Choose the approach that best fits your presentation style.

Speech Rule #4: Practice, practice, practice.

Many speakers prepare a solid presentation but fail to follow through with the essential ingredient: practice. Constant practice separates superior presentations from mediocre ones. It also goes a long way toward eliminating the nervousness that most speakers feel. Prepared speakers usually rely on at least one, and perhaps all three, of these practice techniques: videotape, audiotape, and practice before a live audience. Here are the advantages of each:

Videotape allows you to see yourself truly as others see you. At first it can be a chilling experience, but you will quickly get over the awkwardness of seeing yourself on film. Careful review of the tape, followed by retaping, helps you improve posture, use of gestures, vocal patterns, and eye contact.

Audiotape is a more feasible practice technique for those without access to sophisticated equipment. It particularly helps you discover and eliminate verbal distractions such as filler words.

Practice before a live audience can be done before groups of your colleagues, simulating the actual audience, or before friends or family members. Speaking before such an audience perhaps best approximates the real thing.

Speech Rule #5: Speak vigorously and deliberately.

All listeners expect to be kept interested. Good, relevant information helps, but the enthusiasm with which you deliver it is equally important. Listeners tend to give the benefit of the doubt to presenters who show energy. How much enthusiasm is enough? Here is a guideline some good speakers use. Speak with just enough vigor that the speech sounds a bit unnatural to you—that is, more enthusiastic than you would be in a one-on-one conversation on the same topic. That extra bit of zip is just what the audience needs. After all, you are giving a type of performance. Enthusiasm helps reduce the natural lethargy listeners develop in their passive role as an audience.

Enthusiasm does not mean talking fast, however. Many listeners are suspicious of fast-talking presenters, so speak deliberately, slowing down for those main points you want to emphasize.

Another feature of the deliberate delivery technique is proper use of pauses. Pauses are especially effective right before a major point, such as a main benefit. They can also signal a change from one main point to another.

Speech Rule #6: Avoid those awful filler words.

Filler words and phrases in presentations are like spelling errors in written proposals: once your audience finds a few, it starts looking for more. As a result, your message gets lost. These are the fillers that most annoy listeners:

"uhhh. . . ." (the most common culprit)

"ya know. . . ." (added in the last few decades)

"okay. . . ." (usually abused as a transition)

"uhh . . . mm" (another version of "uhhh")

"well . . ." (a deep subject, as the cliché goes)

How can you rid your speech of these distractions? One technique is to practice before a video- or audiotape machine, as mentioned in Speech Rule #4. When you play back your presentation, you will quickly become aware of fillers that occur more than once or twice. Tape is brutally honest.

Another approach is to practice before a live audience. Instruct listeners to interrupt you when they hear fillers. This technique gives immediate reinforcement. A few years ago as a member of Toastmasters, an international speaking organization, I gave a guest presentation to a chapter other than the one to which I belonged. It is common practice in Toastmasters to count all speakers' filler words. Little did I know that the "uhh-counter" of the Toastmaster's chapter I was visiting regularly blasted an old "Oooogaa" horn from the back of the room at the use of each filler. Though the technique seems crude, it worked. One blast during the first part of my speech was enough to keep the remaining minutes free of fillers.

Speech Rule #7: Use rhetorical questions.

Next to enthusiasm, what vocal technique best captures listeners' attention? Probably the rhetorical question.

Rhetorical questions, like the one in the preceding paragraph, are questions you don't want the audience to answer out loud. Instead, these questions prod listeners to think about your point. They also set the reader up for an answer that you will provide, as in this example: "All right, you're probably asking, just how much will it cost to install these new HVAC systems throughout the plant?" Then, of course, you answer your own question by emphasizing the cost-effectiveness of your product. Rhetorical questions work well for these reasons:

1. They break the monotony of the standard declarative sentence patterns.
2. They establish the expectation in listeners' minds that an important piece of information will be forthcoming.

Use rhetorical questions whenever you want to redirect or regain the audience's attention. They are most effective at the beginning of the talk, at transitions between main points, and immediately before the conclusion.

Speech Rule #8: Maintain eye contact.

Frequent eye contact helps you control the audience. Listeners tend to pay closer attention when you look at them. Here are some ways to make eye contact a natural part of your delivery:

- With small audiences (fewer than thirty people), make regular visual contact with every person.
- With larger audiences, focus on four or five friendly faces in different parts of the room. That way you'll give the appearance that you are surveying the entire audience.
- With any size audience, occasionally look away from the audience to avoid the monotony of intense staring and to collect your

thoughts. Either look toward your notes, as mentioned in Speech Rule #3, or toward a part of the room where there are no faces.

Speech Rule #9: Use appropriate gestures and posture.

Novice speakers have a hard time keeping their body language from working against them, let alone working for them. This is probably why only the most experienced speakers have developed the ability to incorporate appropriate gestures into their delivery.

On the negative side, here are some problems to avoid: hands in pockets, rustling change (remove pocket change before you deliver the presentation), pencil tapping, constant scratching, slouching over a lectern, and shifting from foot to foot.

On the positive side, here are some techniques to practice:

- Stand straight, without constantly leaning on or gripping the lectern.
- Use your fingers and hands to emphasize major points.
- Step away from the lectern occasionally to decrease the distance between you and the audience.

Speech Rule #10: Use graphics.

Today more than ever, people in business and industry think visually. They expect you to highlight your presentation with graphic aids, so don't disappoint them.

Ten Rules for Speech Graphics

A colleague in industry once told me about this incident to emphasize the importance of graphics in the proposal process:

> Several years ago the competitors for designing a large city's football stadium had been narrowed to three firms. Firm A, a large and respected company, had done some preliminary design work on the project and was expected to get the contract. Firm B, another large and respected firm, was competing fiercely for the job. And Firm C, a small and fairly new company, was considered by all concerned to be a genuine long shot. Yet it had submitted an interesting enough proposal to be chosen as a finalist.
>
> All three firms were invited to make ten- or fifteen-minute presentations on their proposals. The presentations by Firms A and B were professional, conventional, and predictable. Firm C, however, took a different and riskier approach. Its presentation was barely five minutes long and given simultaneously with a videotape. As expected, the speech itself stressed the benefits of Firm C's design for the city. The accompanying videotape, however, was quite unconventional. It interspersed drawings of Firm C's design with high-

lights of that city's football team scoring touchdowns, catching passes, and making game-winning tackles.

Firm C's effort to associate the winning football team with its proposed design worked. Shortly after the presentations, the selection committee chose the long shot, Firm C, to design the new stadium.

What is the lesson here? It's *not* that the most sophisticated visuals will always win the contract. Instead the point is that innovative graphics, in concert with a solid proposal presentation, can set you apart from the competition. Firm C had a sound stadium design reinforced by an unusual visual display. Granted, it walked the fine line between effective and manipulative graphics. Yet even the most high-tech visuals cannot disguise a bad idea to a discerning audience. The Firm C presenters won because they found an effective way to present their proposal. They incorporated graphics into their presentation from the start as reinforcement for main selling points.

Speech Graphics Rule #1: Discover your listeners' preferences.

After you have been asked to make a presentation, don't be afraid to ask prospective listeners what kind of graphics they prefer. In other words, apply the same principles of audience analysis to the oral presentation that you apply to the written proposal.

In an engineering firm where I worked, the president preferred the conventional flip chart because of its flexibility and simplicity. Someone trying to gain his support for a project was wise to use this simple device, rather than assuming that more sophisticated equipment was needed.

By the way, when asking your clients or managers about preferred graphics, mention the options available, such as overhead transparencies, slides, videotape, flip charts, and so on. Listeners often appreciate being given a choice.

Speech Graphics Rule #2: Prepare graphics at the same time you prepare your speech text.

Graphics done as an afterthought usually show it. Instead, consider visual possibilities as you prepare the text so you can incorporate them smoothly into your talk. This guideline holds true especially if you have in-house specialists who prepare visuals. These professionals need some lead time to do their best work. Even more important, they can often provide helpful insights about how visuals will enhance the presentation, if you consult them early enough and if you make them a part of your proposal team.

Speech Graphics Rule #3: Keep the message simple.

Most people appreciate simplicity. Moreover, they are suspicious of overly "slick" visual effects that are not matched by substance. In the stadium example, Firm C took a risk by using videotaped football highlights to sell its stadium design. Complex graphics like videotape can sometimes overshadow the proposal itself. Yet in Firm C's case, the tape's purpose was kept quite simple: to associate the success of the team with the potential success of the proposed stadium design.

Speech Graphics Rule #4: Make wording brief and visible, if you use it at all.

The best graphics rely on visual image, not words. Keep them simple by avoiding the clutter of text. Instead, provide necessary explanations during the presentation. When you do need to put words in a visual, perhaps a list of major points, pare them down to the bare minimum. Single words or phrases, like "quality" or "convenient location," can then be elaborated on in your speech text.

Equally important, be certain that all wording is visible from the back of the room. Nothing is more irritating than a poster, overhead, or slide that cannot be read. Prevent this problem by asking beforehand about the room size and arrangement; then adjust letter size and thickness accordingly. Incidentally, standard type is too small to use effectively on overhead transparencies. When using overheads, have the originals typeset in large print or prepared on a word processing system with oversized type.

Speech Graphics Rule #5: Use colors carefully.

Colors can add flair to visuals, but follow these simple guidelines to make colors work for you:

- Have a reason for using them (such as the need to highlight three different bars on a graph with three distinct colors)
- Use only dark, easily seen colors, and be sure that a color contrasts with its background (for example, yellow on white would not work well)
- Use no more than three or four colors in each graphic (to avoid a confused effect)
- For variety, consider using white on a black or dark green background

Speech Graphics Rule #6: Leave graphics up long enough, but not too long.

How long is long enough? Because graphics reinforce text, they should be shown only while you speak to the particular point about which they deal. Reveal your graph while you say, "As you can see from the graph, the projected revenue increases until it reaches its maximum in 1992." Then pause and leave the graph up a bit longer for the audience to absorb your point.

How long is too long? A graphic outlives its usefulness when it remains in sight after you have moved on to another topic. Listeners will continue to study it and ignore what you are now saying. If you use a graphic once and plan to return to it, take it down after first use and reshow it later.

Because graphics require expert timing, you should avoid using handouts. Readers will often move through a handout at their own pace, rather than at the pace you might prefer. Handouts cause you to lose control of your audience. Use them only if no other visual will do, if your listener has requested them, or if you distribute them as reference material *after* you have finished talking.

Speech Graphics Rule #7: Maintain eye contact while using graphics.

Don't let your own graphics entice you away from the audience. Maintain control of listeners' responses by looking back and forth from the visual to faces in the audience. To point to the graphic aid, use the hand closest to the visual. Using the opposite hand causes you to cross over your torso, forcing you to turn neck and head away from the audience.

Speech Graphics Rule #8: Include all graphics in your practice sessions.

Dry runs before the actual presentation should include every graphic you plan to use in its final form. This is another good reason to prepare graphics as you prepare text, rather than as an afterthought. Running through a dress rehearsal of your presentation without graphics would be much like a dress rehearsal for a play without costumes and props—you would be leaving out the parts that require the greatest degree of timing and orchestration. Practicing with graphics helps you improve transitions.

Speech Graphics Rule #9: Use your own equipment.

Someone else's audiovisual equipment almost always seems to break down. New bulbs with a 100-hour life decide to blow, there are no extra bulbs in the equipment drawer, the outlet near the projector doesn't work, extension cords are defective or too short, screens don't stay down—the list goes on and on. Even if the equipment works, it often operates differently from what you are used to.

About the only way to put the odds in your favor is to carry your own equipment and set it up in advance. One of the great false economies of proposal preparation is to spend thousands of dollars to produce a proposal, but refuse to buy a first-class portable overhead projector. This attitude is penny-wise and pound-foolish; money spent on good audiovisual equipment is money invested wisely.

Speech Graphics Rule #10: When you have to use their equipment, have a backup.

Remember Speech Graphics Rule #9, and be prepared for the worst when you do have to rely on someone else's equipment. Here are a few ways to ward off disaster:

- Find out exactly who will be responsible for providing the audiovisual equipment and contact that person in advance.
- Have some easy-to-carry back-up supplies in your car—such as an extension cord, overhead projector bulb, magic markers, and chalk.
- Bring handout versions of your visuals as a last resort.

Remember—you never want to put yourself in the position of having to apologize for inadequate or nonexistent graphics. Plan well.

Example and Critique

Video- or audiotape is the best way to present a speech example, since taping reveals the quality of delivery. Lacking that opportunity, however, we will look at the text of a short proposal presentation and critique it.

Context of Seasled Speech. To show how an oral presentation develops from a written proposal, this speech is based on the formal sales proposal example from Chapter 4. Stephen Wilson, a maintenance supervisor for Hydrotech Diving and Salvage, submitted a solicited proposal to Standard Shipping. Wilson bid on a hull-cleaning and maintenance program for Standard Shipping's fleet of galaxy-class oil tankers. He was betting on interest in his firm's innovative hull-cleaning technology and flexible scheduling, even though Hydrotech is smaller than most of its competitors.

Wilson's bet paid off. Two weeks after submitting the proposal, he got a call from Susan Jackson, an engineer in charge of maintenance. She asked him to prepare a brief summary of the main points of the proposal, to be followed by a 30-minute question-and-answer session. At this point, Hydrotech and two other firms are being considered. Wilson knows they are large companies; in fact, one now has the maintenance contract for all of Standard Shipping's non-galaxy tankers. Jackson also told Wilson about the audience for the presentation. Besides her, the group will include one senior accountant, one engineer in the maintenance department, two managers with business backgrounds, and a senior vice-president who worked his way up from boat captain.

In response to Wilson's question about preferred visuals, Jackson suggests that most audience members like simple, unobtrusive overhead transparencies.

It is clear to Wilson that given the diverse audience, the brevity of the talk, and the preference for simple overheads, he will need to focus on only a few main benefits. Other concerns will come out in the question-and-answer session.

Text of Seasled Speech. After reviewing the written proposal and meeting with his own managers, Wilson prepares the following overview, making sure he can deliver it in only a few minutes. Given the brevity of the speech, he decides to include only a few simple overhead transparencies (noted in the text of the speech and illustrated). He is prepared to hand out much more supporting material, if necessary, during the question-and-answer session.

SEASLED: NEW ANSWER TO AN OLD PROBLEM

At Standard Shipping you have the most sophisticated tanker fleet in the industry—especially with your recent purchase of more galaxy-class ships.

Starts with view from Standard Shipping's perspective, *not* his own

Now you need to give your galaxies the best possible hull-maintenance protection. My understanding is that we're to have an informal question-and-answer

Sets scene by stating purpose, format, and approximate length of presentation

session, after my brief preliminary remarks. I'll take just a couple minutes to outline the present maintenance problem—the fact that it's time-consuming

Lists main points to give listeners mental outline to follow

and inconvenient—and then highlight Hydrotech's proposal to solve the problem with the new Seasled system.

Galaxies have more hull surface below the waterline than almost any other type of tanker. As you've learned in just the few years you've had your

Shows understanding of problem; goes to heart of issue—profits

ships, the process of cleaning and restoring the massive hulls can cut deeply

Uses overhead to focus on two parts of maintenance problem

into profits, for two reasons. [List of two reasons goes up as an overhead transparency.]

- First, conventional cleaning is very time-consuming—the dry-dock method can take between 150 and 200 hours.

- Second, you often must send ships to inconvenient locations for the maintenance to be performed out of water in deep-water ports.

- Time consuming   (Takes 150–200 hours)
- Inconvenient   (Must dry-dock in deep-water port)

FIGURE 9-1   First Overhead Transparency for Seasled Speech

Costs add up quickly, since the tanker cannot be used for almost two weeks. If the maintenance is delayed, even more expensive hull repairs may be required.

Mentions his firm *only* after examining problem

Uses simple Seasled diagram to give physical impression of new technology

Hull-maintenance problems like yours prompted Hydrotech and several partner firms to seek a new method for cleaning tanker hulls. The result was Seasled [Seasled diagram goes up as an overhead transparency]—a diver-operated, self-propelled, scrubbing and painting device.

Seasled can solve your time and location problems in two ways. [List of two advantages goes up as an overhead transparency.]

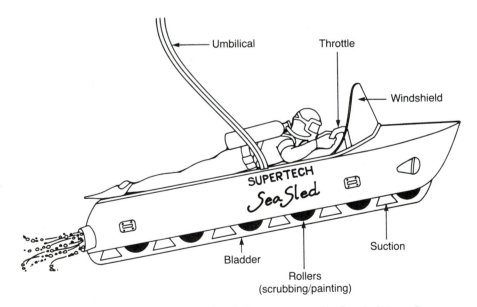

FIGURE 9-2 Second Overhead Transparency for Seasled Speech

- Seasled operates in water
- Seasled goes to ship's location

FIGURE 9-3 Third Overhead Transparency for Seasled Speech

First, it operates in the water and thus eliminates the need to dry-dock the galaxy. You can cut from 50 to 100 hours from the maintenance time. Second, Seasled can be brought directly to your tanker, rather than moving the ship itself to a distant deep-water port.

Gives some details of proposal's main benefits to client

For any non-scheduled work, we can always have a crew on the way to your tanker within 72 hours. However, you profit most from the Seasled system if you incorporate its use into a scheduled maintenance program. Annual cleanings and semiannual inspections are recommended by the manufacturer. We make this program easy for you by keeping a record of each ship's maintenance. Then we'll contact you at the appropriate time to arrange the maintenance and inspection visits.

Returns to main point mentioned at outset—need to increase profits by changing approach to tanker maintenance

Chooses words that reflect client's perspective

In conclusion, Standard Shipping has a maintenance problem that Hydrotech is ready to solve. We helped develop the most advanced technology in the business—technology that can increase your profits by (1) cutting maintenance time and (2) permitting work to be done in the water. And we're ready to start responding to your needs right now.

Now let's move to the questions. . . . .

Critique. Wilson gives a good short speech. He accomplishes his goal of placing initial emphasis on Standard Shipping's two main maintenance problems; then he shows how the main features of the Seasled system can solve the galaxy's maintenance problems. Wilson chooses overhead transparencies because his contact, Susan Jackson, suggested he use them. Note how they are incorporated smoothly into text of the presentation. The speech nicely follows the Preacher's Maxim (see Speech Rule #1) by first telling them what you're going to tell them, then telling them, and finally telling them what you told them. Selective repetition drives home the proposal's main benefits.

SUMMARY

After reading your proposal, clients and in-house managers will often ask you to make a short oral presentation. On it may ride their decision to accept or reject the proposal. Follow these ten guidelines in preparing and delivering your speech.

1. Use the Preacher's Maxim
2. Stick to a few main points
3. Put notes on cards or on a single sheet of paper
4. Practice, practice, practice
5. Speak vigorously and deliberately
6. Avoid those awful filler words
7. Use rhetorical questions
8. Maintain eye contact
9. Use appropriate gestures and posture
10. Use graphics

Graphics are crucial to the success of an oral presentation. These ten rules apply to speech graphics.

1. Discover your listeners' preferences
2. Prepare graphics at the time you prepare your speech text
3. Keep the message simple
4. Make wording brief and visible, if you use it at all
5. Use colors carefully
6. Leave graphics up long enough, but not too long
7. Maintain eye contact while using graphics

8. Include all graphics in your practice sessions

9. Use your own equipment

10. When you have to use their equipment, have a backup

EXERCISES

1. *Oral presentation: In-house proposal*

   Select an in-house proposal you have written during your work experience or one you wrote in response to the Chapter 6 exercises. Prepare a five- to ten-minute presentation that could serve as an overview of the written proposal. Include two or three graphics. Assume your listeners have expressed initial interest in your proposal and now want a brief oral overview.

2. *Oral presentation: Sales proposal*

   Select a sales proposal you have written during your own work experience or one you wrote in response to the Chapter 4 or Chapter 5 exercises. Prepare a five- to ten-minute presentation that could serve as an overview of the written proposal. Include two or three graphics. Assume your clients have expressed initial interest in your proposal and now want a brief oral overview.

3. *Oral presentation: Professional conference*

   Select a product or service with which you are, or can become, familiar—either through experience, academic coursework, or research. Assume that you represent a company that sells this product or service. Assume, also, that you've been asked to deliver a ten- to fifteen-minute presentation on the product or service, with two or three graphics. Your presentation is one of many to be given at an annual conference sponsored by a professional organization in your supposed field. The speech should be largely informative, as opposed to a sales pitch; yet keep in mind that some members of the audience may be prospective customers.

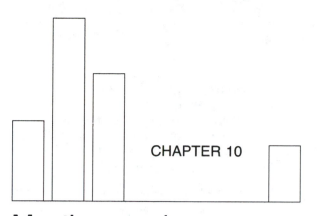

CHAPTER 10

Meetings and Negotiations

OBJECTIVES
- Learn how meetings help the proposal process
- Discover some common problems with meetings
- Learn rules for running meetings effectively
- Become familiar with recent changes in the process of negotiating
- Learn how to apply negotiation tactics to the proposal process
- Practice good meeting and negotiation strategies

Besides oral presentations, two types of interpersonal communication influence the success of proposals: meetings and negotiations. We will focus on (1) meetings with your colleagues during the process of preparing proposals, and (2) negotiations with your clients or managers during their final deliberations on your in-house or sales proposal.

Meetings During the Proposal Process

Most proposals are group efforts, not solo ventures. Chapter 2 describes the storyboard process of planning sales proposals. Effective meetings are crucial during this process. Members of the proposal team meet to review storyboard outlines and visuals generated individually by the team members. Their goal is to give constructive criticism that individuals can then use to write drafts from storyboards. Whether or not you use the storyboard process, however, you have many other opportunities to meet with colleagues in writing most proposals, both in-house and sales. These are a few questions that are often best solved by group discussions:

Does your department, office, or firm have the resources to respond to an RFP?

What technical problems does the proposal involve?

What employees from within the firm will be needed on the project?

Will any outside consultants be necessary?

What specific costs are involved?

Will the project be affected by ongoing work on other projects?

The point is this: because proposals either affect or require help from diverse people within your organization, meetings are a must. You cannot escape them, so you need to know some of the common traps to avoid.

Common Complaints About Meetings

If there is any question in your mind about the importance of running good meetings, do this rough calculation of what they cost your firm. (If you are not yet in a profession, interview a friend who is.)

1. Take the *average weekly number of meetings* in an office.

2. Multiply that number by the *average length of each meeting* in hours.

3. Multiply the result of step #2 by the *average number of participants* in each meeting.

4. Finally, multiply the result of step #3 by the *average hourly salary* of the participants.

The result, which may astound you, is the average weekly cost of meetings in the unit you researched. Meetings cost a great deal of money, yet are often handled in a wasteful and unprofessional manner. Here are a few common complaints:

Meetings start late, often because key members arrive late.

No specific agenda is sent out before the meeting.

When there is an agenda, it is often either unrealistically long or too general.

Some participants really do not belong there.

Conversations are not productive; they go round and round, often without resolution.

The leader loses control.

Participants are not schooled in techniques for reaching consensus; some members dominate, while others do not contribute at all.

Ten Rules for Good Meetings

Considering what is at stake, you have an obligation to make meetings work. As a leader, prepare carefully and provide firm direction. As a participant, contribute your expertise when it is needed and help the leader work toward consensus. Ten basic rules will help create meetings that accomplish their purpose. These rules fall into three stages:

Stage #1: Before the Meeting (Rules #1–4)

Stage #2: During the Meeting (Rules #5–9)

Stage #3: After the Meeting (Rule #10)

Meeting Rule #1: Involve only necessary people.

"Necessary people" refers to only those who, because of their position or knowledge, can contribute significantly to the meeting. Your goal should be a small working group—four to six is ideal. If others need to know what occurs, send them a copy of the minutes rather than inviting them to attend.

Meeting Rule #2: Send out an agenda.

An agenda gives people the chance to do some of their thinking beforehand. And as a leader, you can use the agenda during the meeting to limit digressions. In fact, you may want to attach suggested time limits to agenda items to keep discussions on track.

Meeting Rule #3: Distribute readings beforehand.

Nothing deadens a meeting more than handing out reading material at the meeting for discussion at that same meeting. This method is a major time-waster. If you want participants to review some readings in preparation for discussion, distribute them at least a week before the meeting.

Meeting Rule #4: Have only one meeting leader.

Someone must be in charge at every meeting. Leaderless meetings are like rudderless ships--they almost always founder. Quite frankly, not everyone is able to run meetings effectively. Good meeting leaders must be able to:

- Listen carefully, so that all views get a fair hearing
- Paraphrase accurately, so that earlier points can be brought back into the discussion when appropriate
- Give credit often, so that participants receive reinforcement for their helpful contributions
- Build on ideas, so that diverse points made by different participants work together to form a consensus

Meeting Rule #5: Start and end on time.

Once you show participants that meetings will begin promptly, latecomers will mend their ways. Colleagues who are notoriously late for all their meetings have absolutely no incentive to be prompt if everyone waits for them. More importantly, this practice irritates those who arrive on time.

Setting an ending time beforehand makes it clear that discussions must reach resolution quickly. Most participants lose interest and energy after an hour. Routine meetings should always stay under ninety minutes. Lengthier planning sessions should include hourly breaks and specific agendas with clear goals.

Meeting Rule #6: Keep meetings on track.

Open, lively discussions bring ideas to the fore. As a leader, however, you may need to take control when discussions move off the point. Be assertive (yet tactful) in discouraging these three time-wasters:

- Long-winded digressions
- Domination by a few participants
- Interruptions from outside the meeting (phone calls, for example)

Strong leadership gets results, and results gain you the respect of participants who also want to accomplish the meeting's purpose.

Meeting Rule #7: Strive for consensus.

When possible, reach decisions that all members can live with. A compromise wrought by skilled leadership is certainly preferable to voting on alternatives. After all, you are trying to give all participants a sense of contributing to the final product.

Meeting Rule #8: Use visuals.

As with oral presentations, graphics can help crystallize points for the participants. They are particularly useful for recording ideas that are being generated rapidly during the discussion. You may want someone outside the discussion to write these points on a flip chart, chalkboard, or overhead transparency.

Meeting Rule #9: End with a summary.

Before the meeting breaks up, summarize the discussion and what action will be taken. A summary helps participants get a perspective on the entire meeting and gives them the opportunity to qualify points with which they may differ.

Meeting Rule #10: Distribute minutes soon.

Write and send out minutes within 48 hours of the meeting. If the meeting was worth an hour of the participants' time, it was important enough to record. If discussion items were controversial, have all committee members approve preliminary minutes before final distribution.

Recent Changes in Negotiating

Effective meetings help you prepare good proposals. Effective negotiations help turn good proposals into contracts. We negotiate almost every day of our lives. By choice or chance, we constantly find ourselves in give-and-take discussions to negotiate issues as diverse as

Major and minor purchases

Relationships with spouses or friends

Performance evaluations with bosses or employees

Proposal details with clients or managers

How has the art of negotiating changed recently? In the past, the process was often characterized by words like *trickery, intimidation,* and *manipulation.* In this game's lexicon there were "winners" and "losers" and lots of warlike imagery. Participants, seen as battlefield adversaries, took up extreme positions, defended and attacked each other's flanks, finally agreed reluctantly to some middle ground, and then departed wounded and usually uncertain of who had won the battle.

Today, however, the trend is away from this war-zone approach that demands an "I win, you lose" mentality. As a negotiator, you must enter the process searching for common ground for a very practical reason: Long-term relationships are at stake. In later negotiations, you are much more likely to achieve success if the present negotiation helps both parties. This goal—"we both win"—requires a new set of rules for the negotiation table.

Six Rules for Negotiating

Now that negotiating is so common, you need guidelines that encourage real communication rather than pitched battle. Six rules will help you weave negotiation skills into your personal style. These rules reflect the same collaborative view of business relationships that we have encouraged throughout.

Rule #1: Think long-term.

Enter every negotiation with a long-term strategy. That is the real difference between the old approach to negotiation, wherein the main concern was immediate results, and the new. In almost every case, you need to maintain and nurture the continuing relationship with the person on the other side of the table.

Proposal negotiations with clients or managers have much in common with fairly routine interoffice negotiations. When you evaluate your secretary's performance, for example, there is much more at stake than the percentage raise you give. If your office relies on that person's skill, the most important goal of the appraisal is to build mutual trust; a precise dollar figure is secondary. Likewise with clients, your concern should be the repeat business that may accrue when they believe a contract treated them fairly. The value of repeat business far outweighs a few more dollars on one job.

Thinking long-term, then, is an *attitude* that you project into the negotiation process. The remaining rules for negotiating offer specific techniques for reaching that most important long-range goal of building relationships.

Rule #2: Explore many options.

The negotiating process often begins with consideration of only two outcomes—that is, the specific objectives of both participants (assuming, for a moment, that only two people are involved). You can escape this trap by working to explore many options in the early stages. This technique opens both parties to the kind of creative solutions that satisfy both sides.

Say, for example, that your manager recently approved your internal proposal to add a new systems engineer to your electronic data processing

(EDP) staff. Though exact salary figures were not put forth in your proposal, you now know that an annual salary of about $32,000 will be needed to attract a well-qualified recent graduate in the field. Unfortunately, that figure surpasses by $3,000 the maximum usually offered to entry-level engineers. Your manager tells you that he will approve the additional amount if you secure approval from the manager of human resources, the final arbiter of the company's salary structure.

When you meet with the manager of human resources, he makes it clear that there is a $29,000 cap on entry-level engineer salaries. If you were to immediately respond that you must have $32,000, the negotiation would become a head-to-head confrontation.

Instead, you should temporarily put aside your salary objective. Place lots of options on the table before you allow the conversation to become too focused; for example, you might express consideration for his view and then ask what data are available about the current market for systems engineers. You could then agree to collect some data on this specialized field and meet again in a few days. You might also suggest starting the employee at $29,000 and then adding the $3,000 after a 90-day trial period, offering an early company stock package in lieu of the higher salary. The point is that examining many possibilities keeps both of you talking and getting to know each other's broad concerns, rather than solidifying your separate positions.

Rule #3: Find the shared interests.

If you succeed in keeping the options open during a negotiation, you will begin to discover many points on which you agree. Draw attention to these points of agreement rather than points of conflict. Finding shared interests helps establish a friendship, which in turn makes both sides more willing to reach consensus.

Assume that your negotiation with the manager of human resources resulted in this agreement: you can hire a new systems engineer for $30,000, with a $2,000 increase at six months (if the engineer's immediate supervisor gives an excellent performance rating). In negotiating later with your top candidate, however, you discover that $33,000 is what she expects to receive at the outset. Your goal now is to explore options and find those points—however minor—on which you agree. For instance, you might digress from salary issues to discuss the fact that a proper orientation program should include at least six months exposure to the firm's major technical departments. Other companies with whom she has interviewed may give short shrift to orientation periods. You have thus found a shared interest that can affect the salary discussion. More important, finding mutual concerns can help generate the trust and respect that will keep this engineer working for you years from now, even when salaries may not match up to those of your competitors.

Some argue that the nature of negotiations precludes showing much concern for another's problems—the old "I win, you lose" mentality. In fact, both you and the engineer applicant have the same goal—her acceptance of your employment offer. Building a relationship and finding areas of agreement serve your purpose well, if you have a good case. She may decide she wants to work for your firm, even at a salary less than she could get elsewhere, because you have shown that she will get personal attention at your company.

Rule #4: Listen carefully.

Despite multiple options and shared interests, negotiations usually return to basic differences. An effective technique at this point is to focus on the rationale behind your counterpart's views, not the views themselves. It furthers the negotiation and, in fact, your own case to ask questions and then listen carefully to the answers coming from the other side of the table.

How are we helped by asking questions? Returning to the engineer applicant, when she states her $33,000 salary request, acknowledge it and then ask how she arrived at that figure. Your questions may uncover what is really behind her request. Did her college peers get similar offers? Were these offers from similar firms? Is she aware of the national salary surveys that tend to support your starting salaries? Asking these kinds of probing questions benefits both you and the entire negotiation process in four ways:

- You give your counterpart the opportunity to explain her views (thus breaking out of the attack/counterattack cycle)
- You discover what motivates her (making it more likely that you will find an appropriate response and reach consensus)
- You expose careless logic and unsupported demands
- You move closer to objective standards on which to base negotiations

From your persistent questioning, careful listening, and occasional responses, information may emerge that would otherwise have remained buried. You may discover, for example, that the candidate's friends got higher job offers from firms in another part of the country, where both salaries and costs of living are higher. That would give you the opportunity to introduce a criterion that could help set a fair starting salary: regional differences in compensation.

Rule #5: Be patient.

In the old hard-sell negotiations, participants frequently strived for quick decisions, often to the regret of at least one of the parties. The better approach is to slow down the process. For example, you might want to delay agreement on a final salary figure until after the visiting job candidate has returned to campus, giving both of you the chance to digest the conversation and consider options.

The main benefit of slowing down the process is to prevent basing decisions on the emotionalism of the moment. When objectivity takes a back seat to emotions in any negotiation—with an applicant, a client, a spouse, or a vendor—it is always best to put on the brakes, for two reasons:

- Good negotiated settlements should stand the test of time. When one party feels pressured, mistakes are made.
- Well-thought-out decisions are more likely to produce better long-term relationships, a major goal of your negotiations.

Rule #6: DO look back.

Conventional wisdom has it that once you have negotiated an agreement, you should not look back to second-guess yourself, since it will only make you less satisfied with what cannot be changed. That kind of thinking assumes that negotiations are spontaneous phenomena that cannot be analyzed, which is not true. If you have conducted your negotiations methodically, you will have much to gain from postmortems—particularly if they are in writing. Keep a negotiation journal to review before every major negotiation starts. Besides reminders, this journal should contain a short summary of previous negotiations. Make these entries immediately after a session ends, being sure to answer these questions:

- What options were explored before a decision was made?
- What shared interests were discovered?
- Did you emphasize these shared interests?
- What questions did you ask?
- How did you show that you were listening to responses?

So do look back. Analyze every negotiation to discover what went right and what went wrong during the proceedings. Like other communication skills, such as writing and speaking, the ability to negotiate improves with use. With a few basic guidelines in mind and a journal upon which to reflect, you will discover the power of friendly persuasion.

SUMMARY

Almost every proposal effort involves meetings and negotiations. Along with oral presentations, they are the important interpersonal links in the proposal process.

Meetings often occur during the proposal process. Team-written proposals, in particular, require many meetings during the planning and writing stages. Because many people and much time is involved, ineffective meetings can waste a lot of your firm's money. Follow these ten rules for planning, running, and doing follow-up work on meetings:

1. Involve only necessary people
2. Send out an agenda
3. Distribute readings beforehand
4. Have only one meeting leader
5. Start and end on time
6. Keep meetings on track
7. Strive for consensus
8. Use visuals
9. End with a summary
10. Distribute minutes soon

You often have informal or formal negotiations with those to whom you submit proposals. View these sessions as an opportunity to cement your relationship with your counterpart, to pave the way for later proposals. Follow these six rules to produce an agreement that both parties favor:

1. Think long-term
2. Explore many options
3. Find shared interests
4. Listen carefully
5. Be patient
6. Do look back

EXERCISES

1. *Analyzing a meeting as an observer*

   Ask permission to sit in on a meeting in which you will not participate. Take notes on how the meeting does or does not follow the guidelines in this chapter; then write a report on your findings.

2. *Analyzing meetings as a participant*

At the beginning of a group project at school or work, discuss guidelines for meetings with all team members. Then keep a journal that details the effectiveness of every meeting during the project. At the end of the project, discuss the journal results with your colleagues and/or write a report on your findings.

3. *Analyzing a negotiation: Actual case*

Following the pointers given in Negotiation Rule #6 (Do look back), evaluate a negotiation process that you have personally gone through. Write a report or deliver an oral presentation describing your level of success and the way you followed this chapter's guidelines.

4. *Negotiation: Videotaped role-playing*

The purpose of this exercise is to perform a simulated negotiation and then evaluate the exercise by viewing a videotape of it. Follow these guidelines:

Choose a partner and assume that the two of you are counterparts in a negotiation.

Select a subject upon which the two of you have gained information, either from research or work experience.

Select an evaluator who will observe the negotiation and keep notes on the process.

Submit your written objective(s) for the negotiation to the evaluator before the session, and have your counterpart do the same.

Arrange to have the session videotaped.

Perform the role-playing exercise for 15 to 30 minutes.

Have the evaluator analyze the manner in which the two of you followed this chapter's guidelines, in light of the written objectives you submitted beforehand.

Review the videotape with your counterpart and the evaluator.

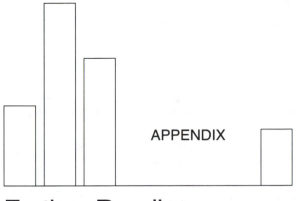

APPENDIX

Further Reading on Proposals

This appendix will steer you toward some helpful books and articles for background information on sales letters and proposals. Although inclusion here does not amount to whole-hearted endorsement, these sources may prove useful in your search for further information on the proposal process. Selections are grouped under three headings: bibliographies, books on proposals, and articles or chapters on proposals. Entries provide a brief description of content and, when appropriate, format. Descriptions are largely factual, though some contain opinions about merit. As you look over this appendix, keep in mind five limitations:

1. Sources concern only proposals and, in a few cases, sales letters. We have not listed sources that deal exclusively with related subjects of editing, oral presentations, and negotiating.

2. Sources are not included on grant proposal writing, which is not covered in this book.

3. College texts in technical writing are not included. Most of them contain an obligatory chapter devoted to proposal writing.

4. Some sources may be out of print or unavailable in your college, company, or community library. If that is the case, ask a librarian to order them from another library through the interlibrary loan program.

5. Sources exclusively on the teaching of proposal writing are not included, since this book is mainly for students and professionals who write proposals, not for academicians.

Bibliographies

Haselkorn, Mark P. "Proposals." In *Research in Technical Communication: A Biblio-graphic Sourcebook,* edited by Michael G. Moran and Debra Journet, 255–283. Westport, CT: Greenwood Press, 1985.

> *This chapter contains a comprehensive list of books and articles on proposals, divided into six main sections: General "How-to's," Specific "How-to's" by Source and Type, Specific "How-to's" by Need, Textbooks and Handbooks, Empirical Research, and Teaching. Sources cover in-house, sales, and grant proposals. Following the narrative is an alphabetical listing of all sources mentioned in the body of the chapter, combined with descriptions that make this chapter an excellent starting point for the proposal writer, proposal manager, or teacher of proposal writing.*

Killingsworth, M. Jimmie. "A Bibliography on Proposal Writing." *IEEE Transactions on Professional Communication* PC-26.2 (June 1983):79–83.

> *Though not as thorough as Haselkorn's bibliography, this article lists many resources under seven convenient headings: General, Education, Evaluation [i.e., the process of evaluating proposals by the government and others], Format and Preparation, Grants-manship, Management, and Style and Rhetoric. Annotations, when they appear, are usually brief; Killingsworth says little about relative advantages and disadvantages of the various sources.*

Books on Proposals

Ammon-Wexler, Jill, and Catherine Carmel. *How to Create a Winning Proposal.* 2nd ed. Santa Cruz, CA: Mercury Communications Corporation, 1978.

> *This book concerns the formal sales proposal, with emphasis on government clients, and discusses basic issues such as technical, management, and cost sections of the proposal. Its breezy format, however, distinguishes it from most other books in this list. Information is easy to find because of bulleted points, writing checklists, frequent headings, and "points to remember" summaries at ends of chapters. Absent are com-plete proposal models to demonstrate the writing guidelines.*

Bermont, Hubert. *The Successful Consultant's Guide to Writing Proposals and Reports.* Glenelg, MD: Bermont Books, 1979.

> *Bermont's book has an unusual format—about 50 unnumbered pages, with only the 14 chapter headings to serve as a road map. Although the book glosses over major issues of format, content, and style, it is still more in the mainstream of contemporary proposal writing than many heftier volumes. For example, it (1) gives solid advice on questions to ask clients before deciding to write a proposal, and (2) stresses the importance of titles and cover letters that attract attention (i.e., that sell). Bermont also emphasizes the need to maintain a natural, concise style and includes two sample proposals with brief critiques.*

Beveridge, James M., and Edward J. Velton. *Positioning To Win: Planning and Exe-cuting the Superior Proposal.* Radnor, PA: Chilton, 1982.

> *Based on a proposal-writing seminar with the same name, this book departs consider-ably from the style and approach of more academic books. It is highly sales-oriented,*

with a main theme of translating features of your product or service into benefits perceived by the client. The authors emphasize that proposals should contain "discriminators"—points that make you appear unique in comparison to competitors. The book offers sound advice on the many stages in planning a team-written sales proposal, but could use more specific, practical guidelines on writing various proposal sections.

Clarke, Emerson. *How to Prepare Effective Engineering Proposals.* River Forest, IL: TW Publishers, 1962.

Clarke's book covers writing of the technical proposal and management of the entire proposal-writing process, with emphasis on the government proposal. With considerable space devoted to many specific and sensible suggestions about proposal formats, the book is closer to a practical handbook than most others. Much of the information is dated, however, particularly that on production, graphics, and further sources of information. Also, there are no complete examples to demonstrate suggested guidelines.

Greenly, Robert B. *How to Win Government Contracts.* New York: Van Nostrand Reinhold, 1983.

Greenly's book is the best source available on writing proposals for government work. It covers the entire proposal process, from initial personal contacts with the client through final negotiations. Although the discussion of technical, management, and cost sections is fairly predictable, the book provides good suggestions on topics often not addressed in other sources. Examples include oral briefings, the "red team" process of critiquing a proposal in-house, the storyboard approach to drafts, and techniques for gathering "intelligence" about the competition. Though basically for background reading, the book does contain some helpful checklists (but no annotated examples).

Guyton, Robert D., and Thomas R. Schaeffer. *Prerequisites for Winning Government R&D Contracts.* Dayton: Universal Technology Corporation, 1970.

The authors survey the process of writing government proposals, from responding to RFPs to negotiating the contract. The book contains an informative description of terms and procedures, but few specific guidelines for writing. No proposal examples are included.

Helgeson, David V. *Handbook for Writing Proposals That Win Contracts.* Englewood Cliffs, NJ: Prentice-Hall, 1985.

Helgeson's book mostly concerns the large government proposal. There is the usual emphasis on analyzing requests for proposals (RFPs) and writing the technical, management, and cost sections. Helgeson, however, breaks out of this mold somewhat by discussing the importance of developing "themes," or selling points, throughout the proposal. The book's style makes it more like a desk reference than many similar books, with checklists and outline summaries to help readers locate information. A complete example to demonstrate suggested guidelines would have made the book an even better reference.

Holtz, Herman, and Terry Schmidt. *The Winning Proposal: How To Write It.* New York: McGraw-Hill, 1981.

More readable than Holtz's earlier book (Government Contracting, Plenum, 1979), this book nevertheless covers the same main subject: solicited proposals for government work. The best features are the passages on strategies for persuasive writing, which note that proposals should "continuously [be] planting seeds of expectation." Also emphasized is the need for engaging headings and visuals: "The less actual reading they [the readers] have to do to understand what you are offering, the better they will like you and your proposal!" One drawback is the prose style; wordiness and sometimes rambling discourse make it hard to locate writing suggestions quickly.

Ireland, Stanley H. *How To Prepare Proposals That "Sell."* Chicago: Dartnell Corporation, 1967.

Ireland's monograph, produced in typescript form with unjustified margins, treats the subject of technical proposals for the government. It describes the bid/no bid decision process, management of the proposal writing process, and criteria for technical/management/cost sections. There is special emphasis on specific forms and techniques a contractor should use before submittal to evaluate a proposal's effectiveness. A sample proposal is included, but little in the way of specific writing guidelines. Some information on format is dated.

Jordan, Thomas E. *Proposal Writing.* Lake Charles, LA: Phi Delta Kappa, 1976.

This short monograph (73 pp.) mostly concerns education proposals, but some check-lists and format suggestions apply to all proposals. Emphasis is on the need to describe as thoroughly as possible the problem the proposal aims to solve. The style is sometimes abstract and jargon-filled (e.g., "proposal instrument").

Larson, Virginia. *How to Write a Winning Proposal.* San Diego: Classic House, 1986.

This book gives a breezy overview of the proposal process. High points are its good suggestions for writing proposal cover letters. But the sections on writing are too brief, even for a short book, and there are no proposal examples. The book touches on some topics that cannot be adequately discussed in such a short book, such as criteria for deciding to bid, management of the proposal effort, and the use of storyboarding. Larson's book is an introduction, not a desk guide.

Loring, Roy, and Harold Kerzner. *Proposal Preparation and Management Handbook.* New York: Van Nostrand Reinhold, 1982.

This useful, 430-page handbook covers both writing proposals and managing the entire proposal process. The authors concern themselves mainly with multivolume sales proposals written by large firms, like defense contractors. The first chapter shows how proposal writing flows from a firm's entire marketing plan. Chapters 2–4 give specific guidelines for the person chosen as the proposal manager. Chapters 5–10 address writing and producing the technical, management, and cost sections, and provide some good advice on visuals. Chapters 11–12 and the appendices discuss topics such as government contracting and provide exhaustive writing checklists. There are no sample proposals. One can ferret out much solid information from this book, but its size limits its usefulness as an on-the-job handbook.

Mandel, Siegfried, and David L. Caldwell. *Proposal and Inquiry Writing: Analysis, Techniques, Practice.* New York: Macmillan, 1962.

Published when big defense proposals were coming into their own, Mandel and Caldwell's book is a primer for writing the multivolume government proposal. There are writing suggestions concerning the usual technical, management, and cost sections, followed by an annotated proposal example. Also includes information on editing, contract law, production, and analysis of RFPs (called "inquiries" by the authors). Some information is dated. Absent are suggestions on now-important subjects like executive summaries.

Society for Technical Communication. *Anthology Series No. 1: Proposals and Their Preparation.* Washington, DC: Society for Technical Communication, 1973.

This volume contains an introduction by Frank R. Smith and 16 article reprints from STC publications. The papers cover a wide range of topics such as proposal formats, management of the proposal effort, methods of evaluation, reproduction techniques, and preparation of last-minute proposals. The articles provide good background information, though some material is dated.

Stewart, Rodney D., and Ann L. Stewart. *Proposal Preparation.* New York: Wiley, 1984.

This book describes the process of preparing large commercial and government proposals. Both thorough and current, it focuses mainly on the traditional technical, management, and cost sections. There are good descriptions of the marketing cycle, proposal management process, current production methods, and the procedure for evaluating proposals. But the book is quite long and ponderous, sometimes including jargon ("profitability optimization") and long, hard-to-read paragraphs. It is not designed to be an on-the-job handbook.

Tilghman, William S. *Your Technical Proposal: A Marketing Approach.* Washington, DC: Data Publications, n.d.

This spiral-bound, tabbed manual (about 45 pages) gives an adequate overview of the sales proposal. Its best feature is the concentration on an important theme: the need for salesmanship, persuasion, and simple language in proposals. Tilghman mainly discusses solicited sales proposals, suggesting a five-part format: summary, problem, proposed solution, management plan, and related experience. No proposal examples are given, and some material is dated.

Whalen, Tim. *Preparing Contract-Winning Proposals and Feasibility Studies.* Babylon, NY: Pilot Books, 1982.

This 48-page monograph introduces the novice to the art of writing proposals and feasibility studies. A few checklists and some illustrations punctuate an otherwise descriptive overview of the proposal process. The best sections survey some strategies to use, and to avoid, in persuasive writing. Whalen's book would be particularly useful to read before starting to write a proposal. Unlike an on-the-job handbook, however, it includes few specific writing guidelines and no proposal samples from either industry or government.

Articles and Chapters on Proposals

Barr, James E. "To Get What You Need—Supply the Facts." *The Balance Sheet* 60 (October 1980): 75–78, 93.

Though directed mainly to business educators writing proposals to their bosses, this article gives writing guidelines that apply to all in-house proposals. Barr states that writers of successful in-house proposals should avoid jargon, make objectives for the proposed change absolutely clear, and counter any anticipated resistance with facts. Also included is a proposal excerpt that follows Barr's guidelines.

Beck, Clark E. "Proposals: Write to Win." *IEEE Transactions on Professional Communication* PC-26.2 (June 1983): 56–57.

As one who helps evaluate proposals for the U.S. Air Force, Beck gives proposal-writing advice from the client's point of view. He suggests that writers of government research proposals should (1) respond to the exact problem described in the RFP, (2) describe any technical benefits that separate the proposal writers from their competition, and (3) be specific about experience that is relevant to the proposal project.

Davidson, Jeffrey P., and Barry D. Rosenberg. "Contract Proposals: Sharing the Wealth with Uncle Sam." *Journal of Applied Management* 5, no. 4 (July/August 1980): 10–11, 31.

In this overview about government contract proposals, the authors provide practical guidelines such as (1) limiting lists in the text to six to nine items, (2) placing illustrations adjacent to related text, and (3) writing technical sections as if the audience were not knowledgeable on the topic.

De Bakey, Lois. "The Persuasive Proposal." *Journal of Technical Writing and Communication* 6, no. 1 (1976): 5–25.

Though concerned mainly with proposals for research grants, this article includes guidelines on style and persuasive writing that apply to any proposal. Contains useful listing of clichés and wordy phrases that often plague proposals.

Dressel, Susan, et al. "ASAPP: Automated Systems Approach to Proposal Production." *IEEE Transactions on Professional Communication* PC-26.2 (June 1983): 63–67.

ASAPP comprises three main parts: the use of electronic boilerplate (standard, off-the-shelf sections) that can be easily produced and revised; a proposal team with clear division of responsibilities; and a five-phase writing process. The article presents this package with the idea that readers can adapt it to the needs of their own organizations. The suggestions on an approach to boilerplate résumés are particularly useful.

Engelbret, David. "Storyboarding—A Better Way of Planning and Writing Proposals." *IEEE Transactions on Professional Communication* PC-15.4 (December 1972): 115–118.

This article presents the basics of storyboarding and its use in proposal writing. Besides describing parts of the storyboard (a two-page module with text and visual, on one theme), Engelbret denotes its major advantages. The article includes one storyboard example.

Freed, Richard C. "A Meditation on Proposals and Their Backgrounds." *Journal of Technical Writing and Communication* 17, no. 2 (1987): 157–163.

Freed argues that a well-written "background" section can provide the competitive edge in proposals. Writers should use this section to explain the history, causes, and effects of the problem that needs solving. A thorough treatment of background information helps the reader understand the need for the proposed solution.

Gilsdorf, J.W. "Writing to Persuade." *IEEE Transactions on Professional Communication* PC-30.2 (June 1987): 68–73.

Gilsdorf describes the features that separate informative from persuasive writing. Sample persuasive techniques include (1) seeking common ground between reader and writer; (2) using both deductive and inductive organization patterns, depending on the reader's expected level of interest; (3) offering the reader several alternatives, and (4) selecting a tone that promotes agreement.

Hays, Robert. "Prescriptions for Using Boilerplate." *IEEE Transactions on Professional Communication* PC-26.2 (June 1983): 60–62.

This article states that boilerplate (standard sections taken off the shelf) has a place in proposals and other technical writing. Using it can speed up the writing process and reduce preparation costs. Hays warns readers, however, that boilerplate poses inherent problems; for example, it can contain previous mistakes that haven't been caught or it may not fit every context.

Ireland, Stanley H. "Preparing Technical Proposals." *Machine Design* 34, no. 15 (21 June 1962): 140–151.

Ireland provides a thorough description of the main parts of a formal technical proposal—summary, introduction, and technical, management, and cost sections. Several detailed checklists and outlines make this long article a more practical writing guide than the author's monograph (see under "Books on Proposals").One useful guideline is that the proposal summary should be no longer than one page.

Jones, Gerre L. "Promotional Tools and Strategy II: Correspondence, Proposals, Job Histories, and Other Tools." In *How To Market Design Services*, 106–115. New York: McGraw-Hill, 1973.

This article offers useful suggestions on writing sales letters and letter proposals. It includes several samples of letters and letter proposals from the architectural and design field.

Kirkby, Peter. "When to Put It In Writing." *Marketing* (18 February 1981): 31–34.

Kirkby discusses both letter and formal proposals, describing when to use each format to sell industrial products and services. Especially useful is the 43-point writing checklist that includes items like this: "Does the proposal begin with a summary . . . for those senior executives who may not have the time or inclination to read the detailed content?"

MacAskill, Robert B. "Persuasion in Engineering Proposals." *IRE Transactions on Engineering Writing and Speech* EWS-4.2 (May 1961): 56–57.

This excellent article offers ten suggestions for making engineering sales proposals more convincing. Both persuasion and technical content, the author argues, must be incorporated into the successful proposal. MacAskill states that proposals should show enthusiasm, adopt the client's point of view, be as short as possible, and respond specifically to concerns the client expresses at preproposal briefings.

Pollock, Ted. "Sales Ideas That Work." *The American Salesman* 26, no. 2 (February 1981): 28–32.

Pollock offers 31 practical tips for writing effective sales letters. The article is meant to relate to sales correspondence in general, but all its suggestions apply well to proposal-

related sales letters. For example, Pollock emphasizes the importance of starting with good openers, using the reader's name in the body of the letter, and writing with the reader's point of view in mind.

Seisler, Jeffrey M. "Proposal Writing: Approaching the Approach." *IEEE Transactions on Professional Writing* PC-26.2 (June 1983): 58–59.

Seisler claims that many proposal writers fail to write an effective "approach" section, which mainly covers the tasks to be performed. He lists the five parts of the approach— purpose, activities, output, anticipated problems and solutions (optional), and timing (optional)—and provides supporting examples from proposals.

Smith, Frank R. "Education for Proposal Writers." *Journal of Technical Writing and Communication* 6, no. 2 (1976): 113–122.

Smith examines the specific writing, editing, and coordination tasks of technical writers who edit large proposals. He then suggests some types of training most appropriate for preparing proposal editors to do their jobs—for example, company internships as well as academic work in basic grammar and interpersonal skills.

_____. "Engineering Proposals." In *Handbook of Technical Writing Practices*, vol.I, 494–579. New York: Wiley-Interscience, 1971.

This thorough chapter covers all facets of government proposals, from assembling a proposal team to writing and editing the technical, management, and cost sections. Its emphasis on government work notwithstanding, the chapter includes many guidelines that apply to all types of proposals. Smith's chapter is good background reading.

Tracey, James R. "The Theory and Lessons of STOP Discourse." *IEEE Transactions on Professional Communication* PC-26.2 (June 1983): 68–78.

Developed by Hughes Aircraft in 1962, STOP stands for Sequential Thematic Organization of Proposals. Tracey examines its major components, particularly the modular two-page format produced through the storyboard technique. The article concludes that STOP's emphasis on text/visual combinations and on group writing still makes sense today.

Whalen, Tim. "Renewal: Writing the Incumbent Proposal." *IEEE Transactions on Professional Writing* PC-28.2 (June 1985): 13–16.

Whalen directs advice to companies who fear losing a government or private contract at renewal time. Chances for renewal will increase greatly, Whalen contends, if companies document the quality work they have done for the clients, help clients write the RFP, and thoroughly analyze vulnerable points.

Woelfle, Robert M. "The Role of the Engineer in Preparing Proposals." *IEEE Transactions on Professional Communication* PC-18.1 (March 1975): 31–34.

Engineers often work on proposal teams with managers, salespeople, publications people, and others. Within this team, Woelfle argues, engineers have some special roles. For example, they must (1) interpret the RFP carefully, making sure not to read into it more than the client intended; (2) write in specific terms about the advantages a service or product will provide clients; (3) be ready to compromise with regard to views of other team members, unless an issue of ethics or technical feasibility is at stake; and (4) write with confidence and a positive attitude, unlike the hedging nature of some engineering prose.

INDEX